East Devon SMUGGLERS' PUBS

Terry Townsend

To my wife Carol

with thanks for her continued

patience, help and support

First published in Great Britain in 2019

British Library Cataloguing-in-Publication Data
A CIP record for this title is available from the British Library

ISBN 978 0 85710 119 8

PiXZ Books
Halsgrove House, Ryelands Business Park,
Bagley Road, Wellington, Somerset TA21 9PZ
Tel: 01823 653777
Fax: 01823 216796
email: sales@halsgrove.com

An imprint of Halstar Ltd, part of the Halsgrove group of companies
Information on all Halsgrove titles is available at: www.halsgrove.com

Printed and bound in India by
Parksons Graphics

Prologue

Here is a window into the world of the East Devon smugglers of old. Men who risked life and liberty to improve the lot of their impoverished families by supplying untaxed goods to eager paying customers. The area of their enterprise encompassed the sweep of Lyme Bay from the River Axe to the River Teign.

From 1680, this expanse of rugged coastline and its challenging interior was the administrative responsibility for Preventive Men based in the Custom House on Exeter Quay. The first half of the story reveals smuggling locations accessible today. Here you can discover contraband landing beaches, smugglers trails, secret hiding places and the grand homes of aristocrats who helped finance the law breaking.

Churches and churchyards also feature significantly as contraband was hidden inside church towers and outside in graveyard table-top tombs. Gravestones and memorials to those from both sides of the conflict are also a rich source of historic information.

During the smuggling era the pub was the hub of rural communities, often functioning as the nerve centre of smuggling operations. Many landlords themselves were involved in the clandestine activities and all were eager to buy spirits and tobacco at the right price. It was in the pubs that plots were hatched, arrangements for transportation agreed and runs commissioned.

Among the featured taverns and inns are some real gems where little imagination is required to sense the desperate days of the men who called themselves 'free traders'. In order to survive, other old hostelries have been greatly extended with a focus on food. At the heart of these favourite family eateries, original rooms with low-beamed ceilings, flagstone floors and inglenook fireplaces are still to be found.

Around the walls in all the pubs are displays of wonderfully evocative photographs capturing the days when roads were unmade and all goods were transported by sail boats and horsepower. In all cases the locations alone offer imaginative possibilities and rewards.

ACKNOWLEDGEMENTS

Thanks once again to Adrienne Bradney-Smith, Robert Smith and Brenda and Tony Stables for their encouragement and practical help.

Thanks also to Rachel Ponting
Archives and Local Studies Assistant
Devon Archives and Local Studies Service
and Campbell Brown, Holcombe Historian

Plus a special thank you to Karen Binaccioni
for her expert contribution with layout and design

TERRY TOWNSEND'S OTHER HALSGROVE TITLES INCLUDE:

Once Upon a Pint – A Readers' Guide to the Literary Pubs & Inns of Dorset & Somerset

Dorset Smugglers' Pubs,
More Dorset Smugglers' Pubs,
East Cornwall Smugglers' Pubs: Kingsand to Mevagissey
East Sussex Smugglers' Pubs
Hampshire Smugglers' Pubs,
Isle of Wight Smugglers' Pubs,
Kent Smugglers' Pubs,
Suffolk Smugglers' Pubs
West Cornwall Smugglers' Pubs: St Ives to Falmouth

Bristol & Clifton Slave Trade Trails

Jane Austen & Bath
Jane Austen's Hampshire
Jane Austen's Kent

CONTENTS

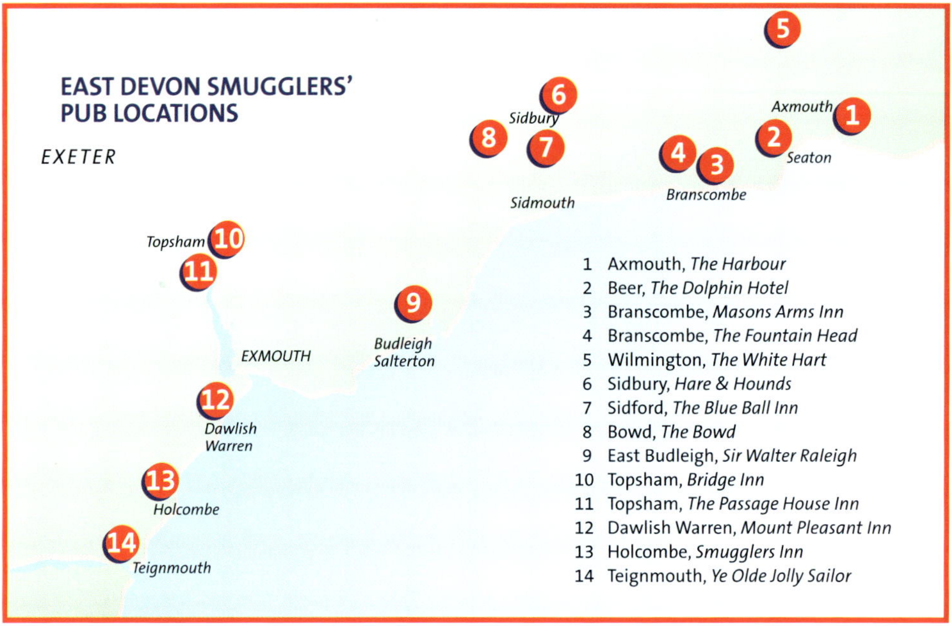

EAST DEVON SMUGGLERS' PUB LOCATIONS

EXETER
Topsham
EXMOUTH
Budleigh Salterton
Dawlish Warren
Holcombe
Teignmouth
Sidbury
Sidmouth
Branscombe
Axmouth
Seaton

1 Axmouth, *The Harbour*
2 Beer, *The Dolphin Hotel*
3 Branscombe, *Masons Arms Inn*
4 Branscombe, *The Fountain Head*
5 Wilmington, *The White Hart*
6 Sidbury, *Hare & Hounds*
7 Sidford, *The Blue Ball Inn*
8 Bowd, *The Bowd*
9 East Budleigh, *Sir Walter Raleigh*
10 Topsham, *Bridge Inn*
11 Topsham, *The Passage House Inn*
12 Dawlish Warren, *Mount Pleasant Inn*
13 Holcombe, *Smugglers Inn*
14 Teignmouth, *Ye Olde Jolly Sailor*

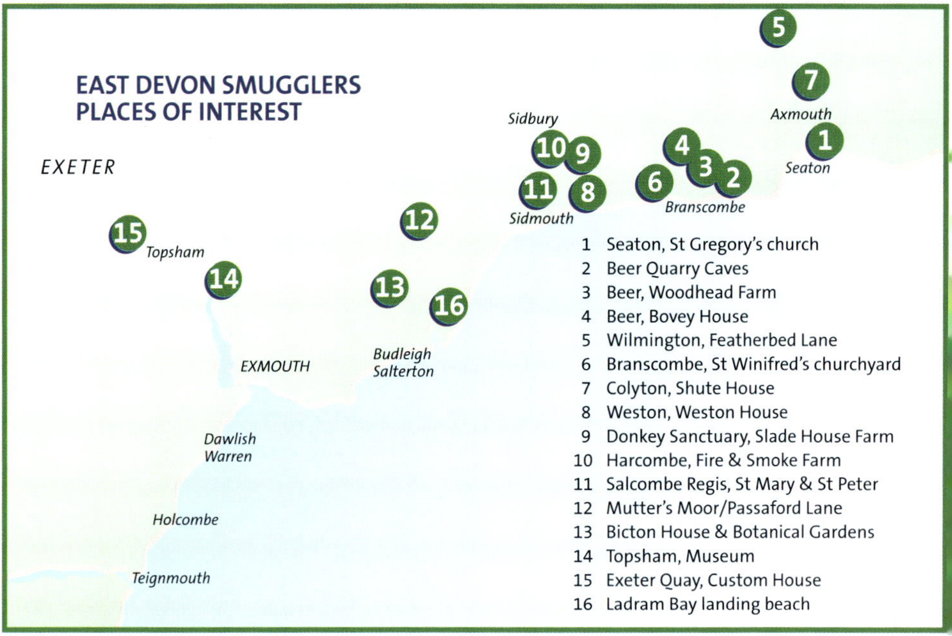

EAST DEVON SMUGGLERS PLACES OF INTEREST

EXETER
Topsham
EXMOUTH
Budleigh Salterton
Dawlish Warren
Holcombe
Teignmouth
Sidbury
Sidmouth
Branscombe
Axmouth
Seaton

1 Seaton, St Gregory's church
2 Beer Quarry Caves
3 Beer, Woodhead Farm
4 Beer, Bovey House
5 Wilmington, Featherbed Lane
6 Branscombe, St Winifred's churchyard
7 Colyton, Shute House
8 Weston, Weston House
9 Donkey Sanctuary, Slade House Farm
10 Harcombe, Fire & Smoke Farm
11 Salcombe Regis, St Mary & St Peter
12 Mutter's Moor/Passaford Lane
13 Bicton House & Botanical Gardens
14 Topsham, Museum
15 Exeter Quay, Custom House
16 Ladram Bay landing beach

Introduction

During the eighteenth and first half of the nineteenth century smuggling became a way of life in England's southern counties. The government itself unwittingly created this situation. When faced with the necessity of raising cash to fund a succession of foreign wars they imposed a high level of duties on a wide range of imported items including spirits, tobacco, tea, silk, salt and many more.

Where there are taxes there will always be attempts at evasion and so began the contest between the law and the delicious deception of smuggling. Euphemistically termed the 'free trade', by those engaged in it, smuggling developed into a huge national industry which the impoverished people of Devon were happy to exploit.

Mention smuggling today and most people think of Cornwall but far more contraband entered the country along the sweep of Devon coastline from Teignmouth to Axmouth with its numerous coves, bays and shrouded river valleys affording excellent cover for clandestine activities.

The county's westerly position, rendering it remote from central government control, also positioned it perfectly for good sea communications with the main suppliers of contraband in the Channel Islands and Northern France, where merchants established huge warehouses stocked full of luxury goods to meet the demand from English smugglers.

Part of the smuggling display in Topsham Museum showing examples of imported items subject to high Customs duties.

The price of a gallon of brandy purchased across the channel was four shillings; the same gallon purchased legally with

To supply the demand for luxury goods from English smugglers merchants in the Channel Islands established huge warehouses like these in St Peter Port.

duty paid could be as much as thirty-four shillings. During the three years between 1779 and 1781 it is estimated that 1,248,000 gallons of brandy and 806,400 lbs of tea were smuggled in through Devon.

Historically famous for its seafaring traditions, Devon had no problem producing the host of skilled sailors, boat builders, fishermen and vessels for this organised maritime law breaking. Devon's peak year for smuggling was 1782 when twenty-five armed vessels of up to 100 tons each, manned by crews of up to twenty men, regularly shipped contraband into the Exeter area.

Contraband transported across the Channel was off-loaded into smaller vessels for landing on the Devon shore. From here the whole enterprise became a logistic tour de force with huge quantities of illicit goods being first concealed then transported further inland to be distributed quickly and efficiently to eager customers.

A waiting smuggling gang could be 70 to 100 men strong and easily outnumber a small contingent of law enforcers. These

Contraband transported across the Channel was off-loaded into smaller vessels for landing on the Devon shore.

men were the first stage porters who carried tubs on their shoulders slung with a rope harness. They were often protected on the landing beaches by bodyguards known as 'batmen' who were armed with heavy staves to threaten or combat interference from Preventive Officers.

The majority of the male working population were not seafarers but agricultural labourers and other manual workers leading miserable lives often trying to support large families. The combining factors of poverty and a thirst for adventure produced large numbers of desperate men willing to flout Customs and Excise duties which were widely regarded as unjust and unwarranted.

Assembling a host of men at the landing place without attracting attention was the greatest difficulty and was achieved by a word of mouth communication chain. Unloading 100 kegs onto the shore and conveying them inland

The first stage of transporting contraband inland often involved porters carrying tubs on their chests and backs slung across their shoulders with rope harnesses.

required 50 men, carrying two tubs each containing four and a half gallons. The whole enterprise from beginning to end was arduous and fraught with danger.

The beaches at Ladram Bay and Salcombe Regis were particularly favoured by Devon smugglers as they were hidden from the prying eyes of the law. The inland rural nature of the county offered many routes for dispersal of goods. Isolated villages, farmsteads, churches, quarries and purpose-dug pits provided convenient front line staging posts. In 1953 Mr Clement Ford, Lord of the Manor of Branscombe, showed Devon author J.W.R. Coxhead six diagonal narrow shafts he had discovered on his land. From skilfully disguised entrances each shaft led down 12 feet to a chamber 10 feet in diameter and could have been created for only one purpose.

A particularly well-used smugglers' trail led up the valley from Salcombe Mouth. Contraband carriers would rest when they reached St Mary and St Peter's church at Salcombe Regis and hide the illicit goods high in the roof of the entrance porch.

J. Y. Anderson-Morsehead noted in his *History of Salcombe Regis* 1894 that:

'The Port of Sidmouth was not in the mouth of the Sid which is Salcombe (Regis) but under the Tunnel Point Rock which has since crumbled back. Hence we never paid port duties and as our clerk old Pike was then blind we used to smuggle our cargoes into the church tower.'

A well-used smugglers' trail led along this valley from the favoured landing beach at Salcombe Regis.

Contraband was hidden high in the roof of the entrance porch at St Mary and St Peter church Salcombe Regis.

This must have been done with the knowledge, if not the complicity, of Reverend Joseph Hall who was vicar here for sixty-three years from 1716.

Beyond the cliffs away from the steep coastal terrain contraband goods could be transferred to pack ponies or donkey carts. The name of Abraham Mutter, a particularly artful smuggler, is still remembered at Mutter's Moor. He owned several carts, a team of donkeys and a number of contraband storage pits just below Harcombe at Paccombe Bottom.

Beyond the cliffs away from the steep coastal terrain contraband could be transferred to pack ponies or donkey carts.

Mutter moved contraband hidden under loads of timber and turf, the products of his legitimate businesses. Wherever possible he took the additional precaution of moving cargoes along the network of hidden sunken lanes.

A Community Enterprise

Farmhouse cellars, farmyards and barns provided favourite hiding places. A mile north of Branscombe, Woodhead Farm had a deep pit behind the cowshed where farmer Samuel Bray used to hide contraband. A small window in the farmhouse provides a view all the way down the valley. Mr Edwin Bray, fourth generation of the old Branscombe smuggling family still lives at Woodhead Farm.

Woodhead Farm, in the hills above Branscombe provided a deep pit behind the cowshed where farmer Samuel Bray hid contraband.

Whole communities were involved and family units included generations of smugglers. In the Sid Valley, in addition to Mutter, the names Bartlett, Northcote and Rattenbury occur frequently throughout the period and can be traced around the area. Most of the local smuggling exploits revolved around tobacco and spirits.

Mr Edwin Bray, fourth generation of the Branscombe family from Woodhead Farm, stands next to the small smugglers' signalling window.

People from all walks of life were involved from the local squire and his lady to lawyers and labourers, bankers and blacksmiths, magistrates and ministers. We are aware of names of poorer free trading families because they appear in Custom reports, trial transcripts and prison records. Less well known are details of the shadowy financiers, crooked clergymen and corrupt public officials.

One member of the gentry we do know about is justice of the peace, Barnaby John Bartlett Stukley of Weston House, Branscombe. He had not been a popular man and many thought he was against free traders, but an old smuggler called Northcote reported:

> *'old Mr Bartlett stored dozens of kegs in his outhouse and you can see the shaft built to let the smell pass out'.*

Stukley's obituary in the *Monthly Magazine* stated that at his death in 1847 he was:

Contraband was stored in the vast cellars at Slade House Farm, Sidmouth.

'said to have possessed property to the amount of nearly a million sterling'.

The year after his death his house at Weston burned down at the hands it is said of an irate illegitimate son who had been passed over in the inheritance. The ruin of Weston House can still be seen, its romantic appearance suggestive of those desperate days.

Further evidence of the gentry's involvement is apparent at the elegant Georgian mansion of Slade House Farm, now administration centre for the Donkey Sanctuary where contraband was stored in the cavernous cellars.

Slade House Farm, now administration centre of the Donkey Sanctuary.

The Preventive Service – Exeter Custom House

The officials charged with collecting duty on imports arriving in East Devon were based at the Exeter Custom House. Built for the city in 1680 this beautiful building stands as centre-piece of the newly remodelled quayside. Remaining in continuous use until 1989 Exeter Custom House is now open as a visitor attraction with displays on the work of the Custom service and the history of smuggling.

The building was designed to accommodate from seventy to a hundred officials employed in the collection of duties on imports and exports. The main focus of the officers was the busy quays at Exeter and Topsham.

Contraband seizures were brought to the Custom House to be destroyed. Tons of untaxed tobacco were burnt in a gigantic stove with an enormous flue nicknamed 'The King's Pipe'. Illicit alcohol was simply poured down a huge drain. As well as casks of brandy and bales of tobacco, tea and silk were among the high demand commodities and smuggled in large quantities.

In her journal titled *Through England on a Side Saddle in the Time of William and Mary*, intrepid traveller Celia Fiennes has left us this description of her visit to the Custom House at Exeter in 1698:

> *'... just by this key is the Custom House, an open space below with rows of pillars which they lay in goods just as its unladen*

Exeter Custom House as it appeared in 1680 with open warehouse arches on the ground floor.

In 1698 Celia Fiennes visited Exeter Custom House and records ascending: '*up a handsome pair of stairs into a large room full of desks and little partitions for the writers and accountants, it was full of books and files*'.

out of the ships in case of wet, just by are several little rooms for Land-waiters, etc., then you ascend up a handsome pair of stairs into a large room full of desks and little partitions for the writers and accountants, it was full of books and files of paper, by it are two other rooms which are used in the same way when there is a great deal of business.'

Customs Officers' 'tools of the trade' on display in the Exeter Custom House.

The Customs Riding Officers

A number of regional Riding Officers were supervised from the Exeter Custom House. The patrol area extended 20 miles east to the River Axe and 10 miles south to the River Teign. Oficers worked on their own, with instructions to summon reinforcements if needed – leaving them vulnerable to attack, or worse. On occasion Riding Officers could call on support from locally stationed Dragoons but the soldiers were generally reluctant to become involved.

For most of the free trade era smugglers had the upper hand over the Preventive Services. Devon's terrain favoured smuggling with its long expanses of rocky, virtually uninhabited coast. With few patrolling Revenue Men smuggling rose to epidemic proportions.

With a great many able bodied men away at war the Preventive Service was frequently undermanned. Those who did take the lonely job of Riding Officer were principally recruited from ex-cavalry men. Although some were gallant and honest, they were continually criticised and many were open to bribery. Lax supervision permitted some to retain their jobs (and the pay attached) until they were eighty years old and beyond chasing smugglers. A number of Riding Officers met their deaths 'falling' from cliff tops.

Customs Riding Officers who were tasked with patrolling the whole coast occasionally gained assistance from small contingents of Dragoons stationed locally.

From around 1800 Revenue Men became more organised and proactive. Smuggled goods needed dropping off in remote coves, and recovering again when the coast was clear. Tunnels and passages were dug out of the cliffs to expedite movement.

After 1831 Coastguards became more vigilant and the old fashioned 'runs' became ineffectual. Afterwards it became the

The tomb of Customs Riding Officer John Hurley in the south-east corner of St Winifred's church-yard, Branscombe. In August 1775 he fell to his death from the top of a cliff.

practice to attach sinking weights to contraband which was sunk close inshore to be collected later. The coastguards' business was to locate it by 'creeping' with grappling irons and claim the prize money.

The Sea Smugglers

Revenue authorities eventually agreed on the obvious course of pursuing smugglers at sea. At first this met with little success since they hired coasters and fishing-smacks whose crews were generally smugglers themselves. The original luggers owned by the smuggling communities were built solely for fishing but, as the activity progressed and free trade rewards increased, some smugglers commissioned fast, purpose-built contraband carrying vessels.

By the early nineteenth century the Revenue Service had acquired some very fine cutters with tall single masts. Often the government wisely commissioned shipyards famous for building speedy smugglers' vessels. Prize money was always the incentive and some cutters with their huge sails were very fast and sufficiently well-armed to tackle any smuggler.

Revenue authorities finally agreed on the obvious plan of pursuing smugglers at sea.

The End of an Era

After the Battle of Waterloo in 1815 the attention of the armed services was directed to combating domestic smuggling. In 1817 the Royal Navy began highly successful blockade techniques and in 1831 The Coastguard Service was formed becoming part of the Royal Navy.

Eventually Coastguards were stationed all along the coast and terraces of Coastguards' cottages are still a familiar sight. This initiative, together with a gradual reduction in taxation on smugglers' favoured goods, saw the decline and eventual demise of the 'Golden Age' of smuggling.

Coastguards were eventually stationed all along the coast and terraces of Coastguards' cottages like these on the hillside at Branscombe are still a familiar sight.

After thirty years at sea as a fisherman, pilot, seaman, privateer and smuggler, Jack Rattenbury published his autobiography: *Memoirs of a Smuggler.*

JACK RATTENBURY

Jack Rattenbury is Devon's most famous smuggler. After thirty years at sea as a fisherman, pilot, seaman, privateer and smuggler, the brave illiterate mariner was persuaded by a publisher to dictate the story of his life. He appears to be a decent man trying to do the best for himself and his family. In the book, *Memoirs of a Smuggler*, published in 1837, Jack gives a good account of his daring exploits as a hardy sailor and fearless swimmer who survived privateering adventures, impressment, imprisonment, shipwreck and storm. A lifeline graph of his fortunes would resemble the profile of a mountain range. At times he was a successful merchant and ship owner, at others he lived a wretched existence languishing in gaol or hounded as a deserter by Royal Navy Press Gangs.

A Revenue Cruiser overtaking a smugglers' lugger off the Devon coast, a very familiar scene for Jack Rattenbury.

Throughout the autobiography Jack reveals little about the smuggling organisations of which he had become a member for fear of identifying former associates. In the end his tantalising revelations suggest a man more stoic than swashbuckling.

A galley of the type owned and crewed by Rattenbury. These hefty rowboats which plied the channel collecting contraband had the advantage over Revenue pursuit vessels because they could head directly into the wind to escape.

Jack was born in the village of Beer in 1778 at the height of Devon's smuggling activities. His mother, local girl Anne Newton, married Honiton shoemaker, or 'cordwainer', John Rattenbury. Jack married Anna Partridge on 17 April 1800. The couple initially lived in Lyme Regis but after four years returned to Beer.

Although Jack lived in Beer he features in encounters at a number of East Devon locations including Axmouth, Budleigh Salterton, Dawlish, Teignmouth and Topsham. In 1896 Sir Walter Besant and James Rice were inspired to write

Bicton House was home to Jack Rattenbury's patron Lord Rolle.

the novel *Twas in Trafalgar Bay*, set in Lyme Bay and based on Jack's adventures.

In the eighteenth century, privateering, a form of government-approved piracy directed against enemy shipping, was an accepted part of Britain's war effort. Ship owners like Joseph Horseford of Weymouth could apply for a licence known as a '*Letter of Marque*', allowing their captains to seize French merchant ships in the name of the King.

Horseford had been part owner of the *Alert* in which Rattenbury had gone privateering in 1800. It was later captured with a cargo of contraband aboard, taken into Falmouth and condemned. Throughout the story of his hazardous career Jack lists at least a dozen occasions when he was captured or impressed into the Navy, but escaped almost as often.

Lord Rolle was the largest land owner in Devon.

In December 1804, to avoid constant harassment by Customs Officers and the Royal Navy Press Gang, Jack decided to go privateering again, joining the crew of thirty aboard the *Unity*, another cutter owned by Horseford and commanded by Captain Timothy Head.

Jack and Anna produced eight children. William, the eldest, joined his father's smuggling enterprise, eventually taking over when Jack was incapacitated by gout. On 30 March, 1836 *Trewman's Exeter Flying Post* published a graphic account of a smuggling fracas thought to have involved William. The incident took place three months earlier on the blustery moonlit night of Tuesday 1 December 1835.

The smuggling fraternity of East Devon had planned an audacious run on the coast just to the Exmouth side of Budleigh Salterton. Towards midnight fifty or sixty men gath-

The entrance to Shute House, Colyton where Jack Rattenbury met with Sir William de la Pole.

ered on the beach. John Batchelor, chief boatman of the Budleigh Coast Guard, spotted a cutter manoeuvring suspiciously and summoned his commander, Lieutenant William Noble Clay RN. With great courage Lieutenant Clay hastened alone to the beach. Beneath the westward cliffs he found a boat ashore and smugglers busy unloading. He twice fired his pistol over the men's heads causing some of them to flee but others came towards him saying, *'Seize him!'* and *'Give it to him!'*. Armed with long guns, pistols and bludgeons they overpowered Clay and binding him hand and foot took his cutlass and pistol before laying in to him. Clay pleaded with the men not to beat him and asked the one he thought was the leader to return his pistol. This was most likely William Rattenbury, who pointed to his own pistol saying: *'This is not your pistol, it is mine, and damned well loaded it is.'*

By now John Batchelor arrived supported by a Budleigh baker named Perriam. The smugglers surrounded Batchelor and grabbed Perriam by his waistcoat putting a pistol to his head. Batchelor stood his ground and fired his pistol and a

Sir William de la Pole of Shute House, Colyton was another of Jack Rattenbury's influential contacts.

blue light signal. Realising the game was up the smugglers fled into the night. John Batchelor untied Lieutenant Clay who, bloodied but unbowed, had the satisfaction of seizing the smugglers' boat with 52 kegs of brandy before going to the station house and firing a rocket to alert the countryside the affray was concluded.

Naturally perhaps such a fascinating rascal as Jack Rattenbury, who could supply luxury goods at affordable prices, was a favourite with the local aristocracy. In particular Lord Rolle of Bicton House and Sir William Pole of Shute House, showed him many favours, doing what they could to keep him out of trouble. It was at their instigation, together with other members of the upper class that Rattenbury, with his unrivalled knowledge of the East Devon terrain, was employed as a consultant in the proposed constructions of a harbour at Beer and a 42 mile extension of the Great Western Canal from Beer to Thorveton.

When Rattenbury was fifty-one Lord Rolle obtained a post for him as crewman aboard – of all things – a Revenue Cutter! After a few months Rattenbury left, citing ill health as his reason:

> *'I returned to Beer and employed myself in fishing, etc, until new year's day when I called on Lord R. He was very angry with me for leaving the cutter. He told me if I was ill he could have procured a long leave of absence, but now he would do nothing more for me. I then called upon several gentlemen to*

Bovey House, a mile and a half northwest of Beer, where contraband was hidden in the cellars, was owned by Rattenbury's sponsor Lord Rolle.

St Gregory's, Seaton where Jack Rattenbury lies in an unmarked grave close to the north-east corner of the church.

whom I was known. They each gave me a new year's gift, by which I and my family were made very comfortable'.

Memorial plaque in St Gregory's church, Seaton to Captain Timothy Head.

Jack Rattenbury died in 1844 and lies in an unmarked grave close by the north-east corner of St Gregory's church, Seaton. Inside the church are two interesting memorials, one to the previously mentioned Captain Timothy Head who died in February 1806. The marble plaque was erected by Head's relation Joseph Horseford of Weymouth. The second, on the north wall is to twenty-three-year-old Midshipman William Henry Paulson who drowned in June 1817 together with eight other seamen during a gale off Sidmouth whilst cruising in a galley HMS *Queen Charlotte* engaged in the prevention of smuggling.

Memorial in St Gregory's church, Seaton to William Henry Paulson.

The picture perfect thatched Harbour Inn is a pebble's throw from the Axe Estuary.

Axmouth

The Harbour

Church Street, Axmouth EX12 4AF
Tel: 01297 20371
www.theharbour-axmouth.co.uk

Axmouth lies on the eastern side of the Axe River estuary, 5 miles west of the Dorset border at Lyme Regis. On visiting the small village today it is almost impossible to believe it was once a thriving port with a large population. Centuries of landslips – common all along this coast – and a build-up of shingle inexorably changed its fortunes leaving it a mile inland from the shore at Seaton Bay.

Ancient ridgeways converged upon the Axe Valley, including a branch of the Icknield Way, and another route, later improved by the Romans, the Fosse Way. In the Roman

Two heavily-beamed bar rooms convey the impression of the interior of a sailing ship.

period, the Axe estuary was considerably wider than today. The river itself was navigable for several miles upstream and plied by the largest vessels of the day. By the eighteenth century the whole area had developed into a busy smuggling centre.

On 11 May 1819 local Customs Officer Richard Broadbridge noticed a suspicious vessel hovering at sea but local smugglers aware of his presence lit a warning fire on the cliff at Seaton Hole. As Broadbridge had previously seen two smugglers cross the River Axe, he made a signal with his handkerchief to alert the men in the Beer Customs Boat entering Axmouth. With the help of boatmen Thomas King and William Simes, Broadbridge secured 28 tubs of brandy, while William Hames seized the boat and its crew.

The arrested smugglers, no doubt regulars at The Harbour Inn, were Henry Partridge, William Newton and Thomas Westlake. All three were taken before the Sidmouth magistrate who sentenced them to six months in Exeter Gaol. To

Refreshment includes Badger Ales, several wines by the glass and the 'all day' bar bistro menu offering a choice of enjoyable food.

Pots hang in the huge brick and stone fireplace with its ancient bread oven.
Below: The pub has been completely refurbished recently although beams and inglenooks have been retained which smugglers of old would have known.

Beyond the dining rooms are comfortably furnished lounge areas.

Broadbridge's dismay they were released on bail and were soon back working his patch.

Sixteen years later the name of Rattenbury appears in Axmouth Custom records. By 1835 the Rattenbury family dynamic had changed and Jack was now helping his son William to retrieve a raft of tubs which the younger man had sunk off the coast between Lyme and Seaton. On 24 June Mr

Across the river and a mile to the west, lies the old smuggling town of Seaton.

J. M. Bate, Chief Customs Officer at Axmouth sent a report to the collector at Lyme informing him he was looking for tubs sunk by smugglers at either Culverhole or Charlton Bay. Bate was unaware the Rattenburys were on the same errand, searching the same area at roughly the same time.

Throughout the eighteenth century contraband was landed within sight of the ancient Harbour Inn.

Working with a gang of Axmouth smugglers, the father and son team used a boat called *The Fish* belonging to Thomas Colman of Seaton, *'an old and notorious smuggler'*. The boat was part of a flotilla of craft legitimately used to transport stone from the Beer quarry caves. That night, during their sea patrol, Bate and his men encountered *The Fish*. It was manned by John Burford (known as *'Uncle Jack'*), John Start and Phillip Garrett, all from Axmouth and Thomas Carter of Weymouth (who gave a false name). On examining the boat Bate discovered a 'creeper' used for retrieving sunken contraband and fifty fathoms of wet rope. He noted the vessel had been camouflaged with paint, making her less visible. Although the smuggling intention was obvious none of this warranted his holding the boat or her crew.

The Reverend Sabine Baring-Gould used Axmouth as background for his smuggling novel *Winefred: A Story of the Chalk Cliffs*.

Accounts of nineteenth-century Axmouth, its smuggling and its cliffs, form part of the background of the florid novel *Winefred: A Story of the Chalk Cliffs* by The Reverend Sabine Baring-Gould:

Axmouth village as the smugglers would have known it.

'The wind from the east soughed about the caves, whistled in the naked trees, and hissed through the coarse sea-grass and withered thrift; whilst from afar came the mutter of a peevish sea. The woman was tall, had fine features of a powerful cast, with eyes in which slumbered volcanic fire. Her cheeks were ushed, her rich, dark hair, caught by the wind and sopped by the mist, was dishevelled under her battered hat. She was not above thirty-six years old'.

The welcoming Harbour Inn in picturesque Axmouth, a pebble's throw from the Axe Estuary is a popular place for walkers and birdwatchers to refuel. The Grade II listed thatched seventeenth-century building features two heavily beamed bar rooms and two dining rooms also retain heavy beams and a snug alcove. The walls are decorated throughout with prints of nautical scenes.

Badger Ales and several wines by the glass complement the 'all day' bar bistro menu offering a choice of enjoyable food from local butchers' ham sandwiches to Poachers Ale Pie. Don't forget to leave room for apple and blackberry oat crunch crumble and custard. Children and dogs are welcome in the bar area and outside, where there is modern furniture on the terrace and picnic-sets on the lawn.

Beer

The Dolphin Hotel

Fore Street, Beer, Devon EX12 3EQ

Tel: 01297 20068

www.dolphinhotelbeer.co.uk

The majestic chalk cliffs of England's south coast appear for the last time where the great bulk of Beer Head rises high over the maritime scene, offering westerly protection to a fishing village of immense charm. In consequence the beach is a natural suntrap and the waters of the bay are very sheltered. If you like cliff-top walks with superb sea views, you'll be spoilt for choice.

Because Beer has a 'working beach' the picturesque paraphernalia of the fishing industry with its brightly coloured wooden boats, nets, winches and vibrantly-hued floats add to the charm. There is also the bonus of watching fishermen landing their catches of fresh fish, crabs, lobsters and scallops. In the late eighteenth century and early nineteenth century,

The seventeenth-century 'Long Bar' with its white painted façade, now incorporated as part of the later Dolphin Hotel.

The old village road smugglers would have known passes The Dolphin and leads directly down to the shore.

smuggling provided many poor fisherfolk of Beer with an additional income opportunity. George Pulman in *The Book of the Axe*, published in 1875, says:

> *'In former days, when the coastguard was inefficient and the exciseman lax, the Beer men were the very kings of smugglers'.*

Beer fishermen always had a fine reputation handling sail boats. Their 'luggers' were 25ft to 35ft in length, built in Beer and usually manned by a crew of four. Their seafaring skill combined with the ideal geographical location for landing contraband and transporting it to remote farms and houses inland contributed to the proliferation of 'free trade'. By 1750, the area was so notorious the local Revenue Officers were reinforced by Dragoons quartered in Beer, Branscombe and Seaton.

Three West Country ales are always on tap.

As previously mentioned, Jack Rattenbury, Beer's most famous fisherman turned smuggler, was born in the village in 1778. Encouraged by a publisher and helped by a local

At the far end of the Long Room is an area for table skittles, darts and pool. Live music events are hosted here through June to September.

Unitarian clergyman, Jack was persuaded to write about his adventures. *Memoirs of a Smuggler* was published in 1837 in which Jack gave a good account of his own daring exploits. The publisher, with an eye to sales, dubbed him the '*Rob Roy of the West*'.

In 1808 Rattenbury became landlord of an inn or beerhouse in Beer which could well have been the seventeenth-century 'Long Bar' with its white-painted façade, now incorporated as part of the later Dolphin Hotel. In any event he would certainly have frequented this pub.

In his book Jack writes of an encounter that took place in Beer in November 1808. Following a smuggling trip to Alderney, he went to a public house in Beer for a drink when Sergeant Hill of the South Devon Militia attempted to arrest him for desertion from the Royal Navy. Rattenbury admits he was terrified because punishment for desertion was three hundred lashes of a cat o'nine tails, delivered 25 at a time in front of the crew of every

Jack Rattenbury had a narrow escape when Sergeant Hill of the South Devon Militia attempted to arrest him for desertion from the Royal Navy.

The sheltered beach is protected by the majestic cliffs of Beer Head.

A small heritage centre on the promenade tells the story of Jack Rattenbury's life and adventures.

ship in the fleet. Whilst trying to persuade the Sergeant he had the wrong man Jack jumped down into the pub cellar through an open trap door, discarding his jacket and shirt so the soldiers could not grab hold of him.

> *'Having armed myself with a reap hook, and with the knife I had in my pocket, I threw myself into an attitude of defense at the cellar's entrance. "I won't be taken from this spot alive" I declared. "I'll kill the first man who comes near me".'*

Sergeant Hill ordered his men to advance on Jack and seize him but they replied: *"You proposed it, so you take the lead. Set an example and we will follow"*. After a four-hour standoff Jack made his escape by pushing through the soldiers who were momentarily distracted by a woman rushing into the room crying a boy was in danger of drowning.

The quarry caves were the perfect location for local smugglers to conceal large quantities of contraband.

Beer Quarry Caves resulted from 2000 years of quarrying beer stone and today are a popular visitor attraction.

The earliest record of the Dolphin appears in 1774, four years before Rattenbury's birth. At that time it was described as part of a small farm held by Jacob Bonner and listed under the name Micho's which included the Dolphin orchard.

The present day Dolphin Hotel offers the best of both worlds. There is a spacious, relaxed lounge bar and restaurant in the hotel section while the Long Bar caters more for local drinkers and the family holiday trade. Table skittles, darts, pool, digital juke box and two fruit machines are provided and live music events are hosted through June to September.

A perfect summer scene at th
Masons Arms, Branscombe.

Branscombe
Masons Arms Inn

Branscombe Village, Branscombe EX12 3DJ

Tel: 01297 680300

www.masonsarms.co.uk

While the nearby fishing port of Beer was the undisputed smuggling capital of East Devon, Branscombe played a part in the nightly cat-and-mouse game with Customs Men which reached its height during the time of the Napoleonic Wars. It wasn't only spirits that were smuggled along this part of the coast. Among more unusual items were French burrstones, used for fine grinding. Manufactured in the Marne Valley in northern France they were highly prized as the finest mill-stones and subject to a heavy duty.

A contemporary account of smuggling in Branscombe by

The rambling main bar of the Masons Arms incorporates ancient ships' beams and a log fire in a massive hearth.

Below: The pub is a popular pit stop for cyclists and walkers along the South West Coast Path.

George Pulman, published in 1857, highlights what men like John Hurley the local Riding Officer were up against:

> *'... smugglers could [not] have been much in dread of the exciseman for, when a child, I have often met strings of their horses by daylight, in charge of only a single person, travelling along the secluded roads and heavily laden with the contraband. The smugglers' horses were all remarkably sagacious. They travelled in single file, eight or ten together, and one of them – the oldest and most experienced – was called the Captain. He led the rest, and they all knew the 'enemy' and how to treat him. It was dangerous to attempt to stop them and, truth to tell, the experiment was seldom tried.'*

St Austell Proper Job and Tribute along with Otter Bitter and guest beers such as Branscombe Vale's 'Summa This' are on hand pump.

There were periods when Customs Men were assisted by the army. In 1747 small contingents of soldiers were based in the most dangerous places. A commander and eight men were stationed at Beer, a sergeant and six men at Sidmouth, four men at Seaton and four at Branscombe. The steady trade in

Comfortable seats, chairs and settles stand on slate floors.

illegal imports and exports continued but during these times it took place mostly at night and in great secrecy, involving the hollow hedges, sunken tubs and diversionary tricks.

This old pub is ultimately and appropriately dog friendly.

There was a known contraband hiding pit at Woodhead Farm. The old thatched farmhouse with modern extension is set high above the Branscombe Valley, at the brow of steep Seller's Wood Hill leading up from the Masons Arms. From a small ground floor window there is a view down the valley and on landing nights, if Customs Men were known to be patrolling, a light was placed here as a warning to the contraband carriers.

According to Henry Northcote, born in 1819, two Branscombe farmers, Bray and Fry, were the mainstays of local smuggling. Samuel Bray of Woodhead Farm north of Branscombe concealed contraband in a deep pit behind the cowshed. The entrance to the store, which was never discovered by the authorities, was covered by tree trunks and a hayrick.

Strict Penalties for assisting smugglers included fines, imprisonment or even transportation. The great-great-great uncle of Edwin Bray, the present owner of Woodhead Farm, spent time in gaol on smuggling offences. A Customs Cottage still remains in Branscombe village and during the nineteenth century, the Branscombe Mouth lookout was built to house up to half a dozen Customs Men.

The Masons Arms was originally a cider house amidst a small terrace of cottages. Today the pub occupies the whole row and has been extended at the rear. Hostelries that have grown progressively like this are among the most interesting to explore. For centuries the whole village was owned by the Dean and Chapter of Exeter Cathedral and it is said the pub was named after the masons who built that great church using stone from the nearby quarries.

Today the rambling main bar of the Masons Arms is the heart of the pub with ancient ships' beams and a log fire in a massive hearth. This is where dry-throated quarry workers slaked their thirst while discussing coercive plans for concealing contraband with the local fishermen smugglers. Comfortable seats, chairs and settles stand on slate floors in this and a second bar while two smartly furnished dining rooms complete a very satisfying experience.

The Masons Arms at Branscombe in 1901 as smugglers would have known it.

St Austell Proper Job and Tribute along with Otter Bitter and guest beers such as Branscombe Vale's 'Summa This' are on hand pump, complemented by ten wines by the glass. A quiet flower-filled front terrace, with thatched-roof tables, extends into a side garden. The sea with its former smuggling landing beach is just a stroll away through the pretty village.

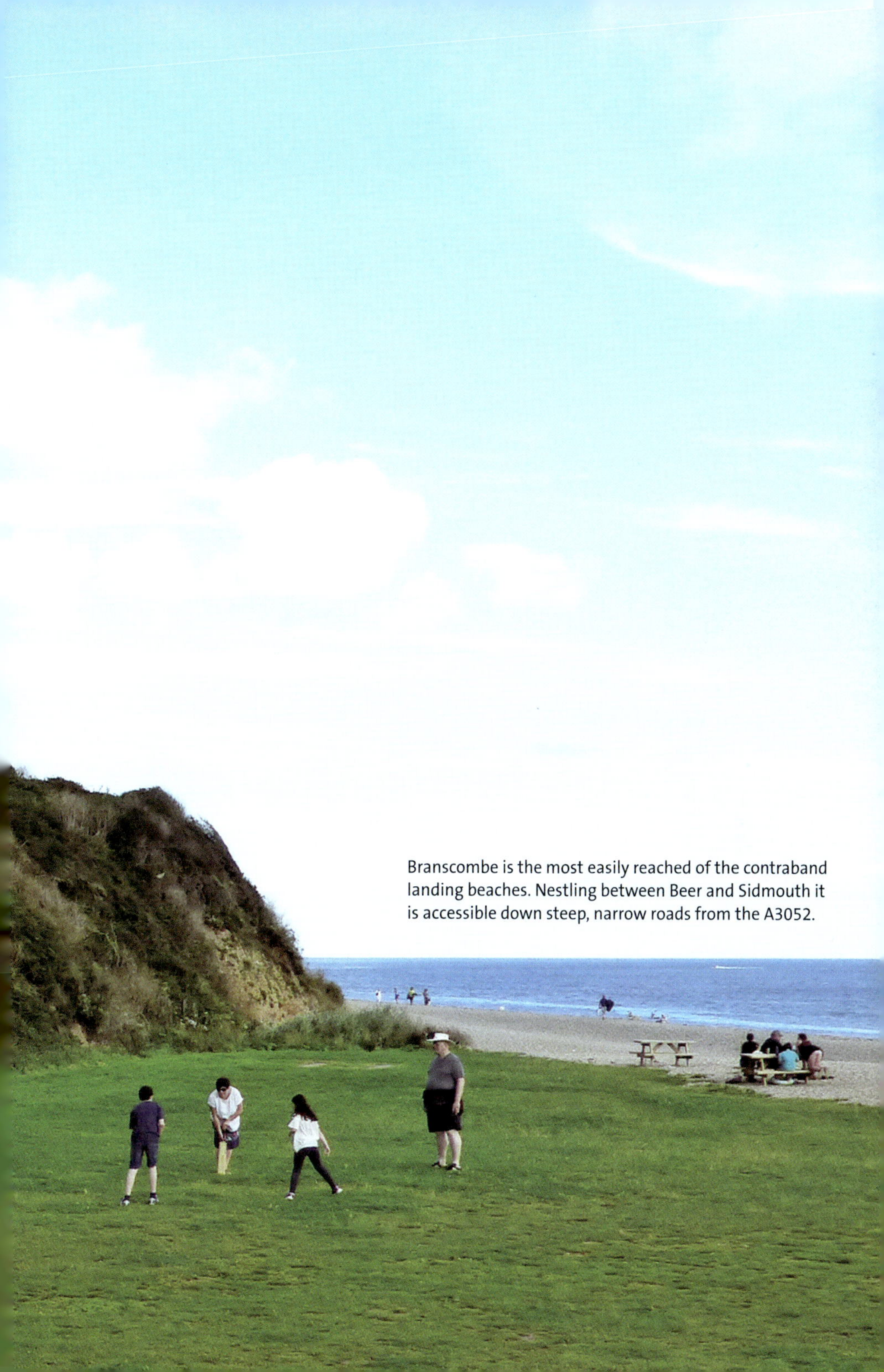

Branscombe is the most easily reached of the contraband landing beaches. Nestling between Beer and Sidmouth it is accessible down steep, narrow roads from the A3052.

Branscombe

The Fountain Head

Branscombe, Seaton EX12 3BG

Tel: 01297 680359

www.fountainheadinn.com

Aerial photographs on display in The Fountain Head appear to support the claim that Branscombe is the longest village in Britain snaking for more than a mile along a deep valley. At its western end lies a hamlet of thatched cottages and, at a confluence of underground streams, the fourteenth-century Fountain Head nestles beside a former smugglers' trail. Now a bridle path, the trail passes directly in front of the Fountain Head through the pub's terrace garden.

Just a very warm welcome and everything that pubs used to be. It is easy to see why many regard The Fountain Head as one of Devon's finest inns.

Halfway along the rising lane St Winifred's church appears on the left with its splendid view down the valley. For over two hundred and sixty years a box tomb in the south-east corner of the churchyard has marked the last resting place of a brave Customs Officer.

The old smugglers' trail led directly through what is now the pub's terrace garden.

In the early days of 'free trading' smugglers had it very much their own way. Their main opposition came from the local Customs Official who held the post of Riding Officer. These men, usually retired cavalry officers, were recruited from the area to which they were assigned. As smuggling was a large part of the local economy involving most of the villagers Riding Officers became social outcasts even among their own family and friends.

It was a very lonely vocation, riding out every night in all weathers for hours at a time looking for suspicious activity, not knowing if they would return home safely. Not only was it poorly paid it was also an extremely dangerous job often resulting in the officer being severely beaten or even murdered. If a Riding Officer did confront a crowd of smugglers, he was often the loser. It is not surprising to learn they were often prepared to accept bribes to be elsewhere when a contraband run was expected.

There are no electronic games; pool tables, wide screen televisions or intrusive music.

Below: A wonderfully evocative collection of old photographs is displayed around the walls.

An endangered dartboard, with tyre surround still hangs on the wall and dog biscuits and local fudge are sold at the bar.

In August 1755 John Hurley, the Riding Officer at Branscombe, fell to his death over 'White Cliff' in circumstances which indicated all too clearly the dangers any conscientious officer faced. The inscription on his tomb, now almost illegible, explains how he died:

> *'Here lieth the body of Mr John Hurley, Custom House Officer of this parish. As He was endeavouring to extinguish some Fire made between Beer & Seaton as a signal to a Smuggling Boat then off at Sea He fell by some means or other from the Top of the Cliff to the bottom by which He was unfortunately Killed.'*

The three bitters on tap are from the nearby Branscombe Vale Brewery.

Hurley was only forty-five and his annual salary a mere £35. The coroner's verdict was accidental death.

This 500-year-old former forge and cider house is a true rural survivor, in a peaceful village a short walk from the coast

The former blacksmith's shop now serves as the dining room.

path. The traditional worn flagstones, crackling log fires, rustic furnishings, village-brewed beers from Branscombe Vale, and the chatty atmosphere charm both locals and visitors.

The original forge is incorporated as a feature inside this wonderful old inn.

In the small, snug interior tankards hang expectantly from beams. An endangered dartboard, with tyre surround still hangs on the wall, and dog biscuits and local fudge are sold at the bar. The collection of old photographs on display is an additional delight. One taking pride of place above the fireplace is the most evocative of all. It was taken around 1900 and shows landlord Thomas Gill receiving a delivery from the butcher's van. The lady in the centre is probably Mrs Gill in the process of making tea for two visiting cyclists; the second bicycle must belong to the photographer. The figure on the left is the resident blacksmith. In a few years all of these people will be visited by the horrors of the First World War.

Rabbit stew was a popular economic dish and another picture shows a former landlord with his dog, shotgun and ferret box off to bag a few for the pot. A further photograph shows a farmhand leading a horse to the forge for shoeing. This last picture was taken in 1920 by which time the thatch roof of the old forge had been replaced by pantiles. The blacksmith being observed by a small group of boys was the last Fountain Head farrier, Jimmy Loveridge.

This photograph from around 1900 shows landlord Thomas Gill receiving a delivery from the butcher's van whilst his wife makes tea for two visiting cyclists. The figure on the left of the group is the blacksmith.

The menu includes a selection of perennial home cooked favourites that won't break the bank including chicken liver pâté, steak and kidney pie, rack of lamb, Cajun spiced chicken breast, parsnip mash, caramelised red onion, wild mushrooms with red wine dressing and the freshest of fresh crab sandwiches.

A former landlord with his dog, shotgun and ferret box off to bag a few rabbits for the pot.

Farmers bringing their horses to be shod enjoyed the opportunity of quaffing a glass or two of cider while they waited.

The pub's ancient flagstones slope just enough to cause some customers to wonder about the mythical effects of traditional farmhouse cider, in this case piercingly dry Thatchers Cheddar Valley and Countryman from Tavistock. Real ales, including the comically named 'Hells Belles', full-bodied 'Summa' That' and the light, quaffable 'Branoc', all from the nearby Branscombe Vale Brewery.

Not many pubs like the Fountain Head remain. This is a place to enjoy some good conversation, to sup some ale and relax. There are no electronic games; pool tables, wide screen televisions or intrusive music. Just a very warm welcome and everything that pubs used to be. It is easy to see why many regard this as one of Devon's finest inns.

This photograph taken around 1920 shows Jimmy Loveridge, the last working blacksmith, standing outside the forge.

Wilmington

The White Hart

Wilmington, Honiton EX14 9JQ

Tel: 01404 831053

Since the fifteenth century Wilmington has sat astride the former main route from Exeter to London, mid-way between Honiton and Axminster. In the centre of the village this roadside inn was originally known as 'The Wheelers House' and earliest records of landlords show John Cooks succeeded Thomas Shoppard in 1736. Over the following decades the village became a smuggling hub, providing numerous tub carriers for free traders of Branscombe and Beer, 7 miles due south.

The early importance of the road was confirmed in 1765 when it became the Honiton to Axminster Turnpike, evolving into the present busy A35. In 1805 the village street rang to the clatter of galloping horses as messengers racing to London

This roadside pub in the centre of the village was known originally as 'The Wheelers House'.

Very experienced chef John House has formed a winning partnership with established landlady Margaret Bolt.

with news of the Battle of Trafalgar changed their mounts at 'The Wheelers House'. In 2005 this historic event was marked by the unveiling of a plaque placed on the inn recording details of the messengers and honouring local men who fought at the battle.

Early in the nineteenth century the Old London Road (known today as Trafalgar Way) had been superseded by the A30/A303, providing a more direct route to the capital over the Blackdown Hills. In 1850 when Thomas Kibby was landlord of the Wilmington pub the name was changed to The White Hart Inn.

Evidence of smuggling days hereabouts can still be seen on a couple of village buildings. Free traders embedded a bottle

Superior quality freshly-cooked food is served all day in the well-planned bar and restaurant.

high on the flank wall of a cottage so just the bull's-eye end was visible. This coded message indicated the place was a safe house for smugglers.

In 1953 a descendant of a local smuggler described how his grandfather had helped land cargoes. Tubs were off-loaded to a particularly inaccessible beach at the base of a 400 foot cliff close to Branscombe and Salcombe Regis. The tub men then appeared at the cliff top with long ropes attached to a farm gate. Using the gate as a platform one man was lowered to the beach, where he loaded the gate with tubs and was hoisted up again. This system was not foolproof and on at least one run, a rope broke or became detached and the brave smuggler fell to his death on the rocks below.

The old smugglers would still recognise the front section of the thatched White Hart Inn, with its thick cob walls.

During the smuggling era a sunken track, still known locally as 'Featherbed Lane', led up from the coast at Seaton joining

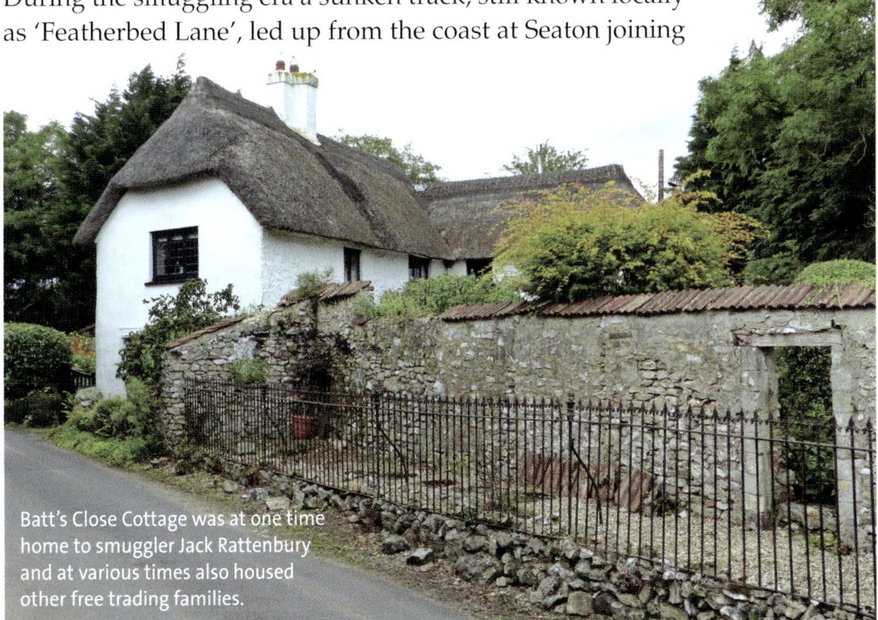

Batt's Close Cottage was at one time home to smuggler Jack Rattenbury and at various times also housed other free trading families.

This bull's-eye bottle end under the thatched eaves of Batt's Close cottage signified the owner was sympathetic to smugglers.

the London Road between Wilmington and Offwell, alongside a cottage called 'Batt's Close'. Although the lane has been developed for much of its length, a section of sunken track can still be seen close by.

Batt's Close Cottage was once home to smuggler Jack Rattenbury and at various times also housed other free trading families. At first glance it appears attractive but unexceptional, built in a style typical of much Devon vernacular architecture. However, looking more closely just below the thatched eaves, reveals the telltale glass bull's-eye bottle end.

Featherbed Lane joins the original smugglers' trail a little way beyond Batt's Close.

At Wilmington, a little way down the road diagonally across from the pub, is another bottle sign in the eastern gable end of School House Cottage. There used to be an old chapel in the cottage garden where a rudimentary education was provided for village children. In Victorian times a purpose-built school was erected next to the cottage and now serves as the village hall.

This cottage had an old chapel in the garden where a rudimentary education was provided for village children.

Today only the front section of the thatched White Hart Inn, with its thick cob walls, would be recognisable to smugglers of old. The remainder was rebuilt after a major fire in 2004. Despite the trauma the pub retains an authentic country atmosphere with a friendly welcome.

Very experienced chef John House has formed a winning partnership with established landlady Margaret Bolt. Superior quality freshly-cooked food at affordable prices is served all day in the well-planned bar and restaurant. Tempting choices include home-made lasagne, tuna pasta bake and large west country gammon steaks.

Diagonally across the road from the pub the bottle sign on the gable end of School House Cottage is still clearly visible.

Sidbury

Hare & Hounds

Putts Corner EX10 0QQ

Tel: 01400 41760

www.hareandhounds-devon.co.uk

The ancient crossroads at Putts Corner lies a couple of miles south of Honiton on the A375. There, in the shrubbery hard by the Hare & Hounds, is the 'Witches Stone' or 'Slaughter Stone' to which numerous folklore legends are attributed. The collective will to move stones of this size existed only in the Neolithic and Bronze Age periods.The area and the pub have an exciting and lurid past. Due to its isolation it was a popular haunt for poachers and smugglers. In 1787 two Excise Men were killed by a gang of smugglers at Roncombe Gate, less than 2 miles west of Putts Corner. On 29 November this announcement appeared in *Trewman's Exeter Flying Post*:

The Hare & Hounds, previously known as Hunters Lodge, has an exciting and lurid past.

The inglenook with its bread oven is a focal point in the bar. **Below:** Interior clues to the former smugglers' pub include original beams and some massively thick walls.

Besides the daily carvery, th
extensive menu features cl
pub dishes and snacks serv
the spacious, airy dining ro

The permanent cask ales are brewed less than 10 miles away at Ottery Brewery.

'Whereas it has been humbly represented to the King, that on Friday Evening, the 2nd Day of November Instant, a most inhuman Murder was committed on the bodies of William Jenkins and William Scott, late Officers in his Majesty's Excise, by a Gang of Smugglers, when the said officers were in the Execution of their Duty, in attempting to seize some Run Goods, at a Place called Roncombe Girt [Gate].'

William Voisey was named as one of the murderers, and a pardon was promised to the smuggler who supplied the names of Voisey's accomplices, with a further inducement of £200 paid on conviction. Half a century later matters had not improved. In 1836 newspapers reported details of a prosecution for assault against two Preventive Officers, Lieutenant William Noble Clay, Chief Officer of the Coastguard at Budleigh Salterton, and his chief boatman, John Batchelor.

The attack had taken place at Budleigh on 1 December 1835 when a party of smugglers involved in landing 52 kegs of spirits was challenged by Customs Men. The case was brought against none other than Jack Rattenbury's son William, also Henry Bird, another smuggler from the hamlet of Buckerell west of Honiton.

Customs officials spotted a suspicious cutter at midnight and following this up they disturbed a band of armed smugglers on the beach. The lieutenant had been surrounded by eight free traders who tied his arms and legs and beat him. All his boatmen were driven off except Batchelor who tried to go for help but was himself attacked.

Details of the court case suggest some doubt as to the smugglers' identity and because they were past offenders it seems

The spacious family-friendly garden.

From the garden there are spectacular views all the way down the valley to the sea at Sidmouth.

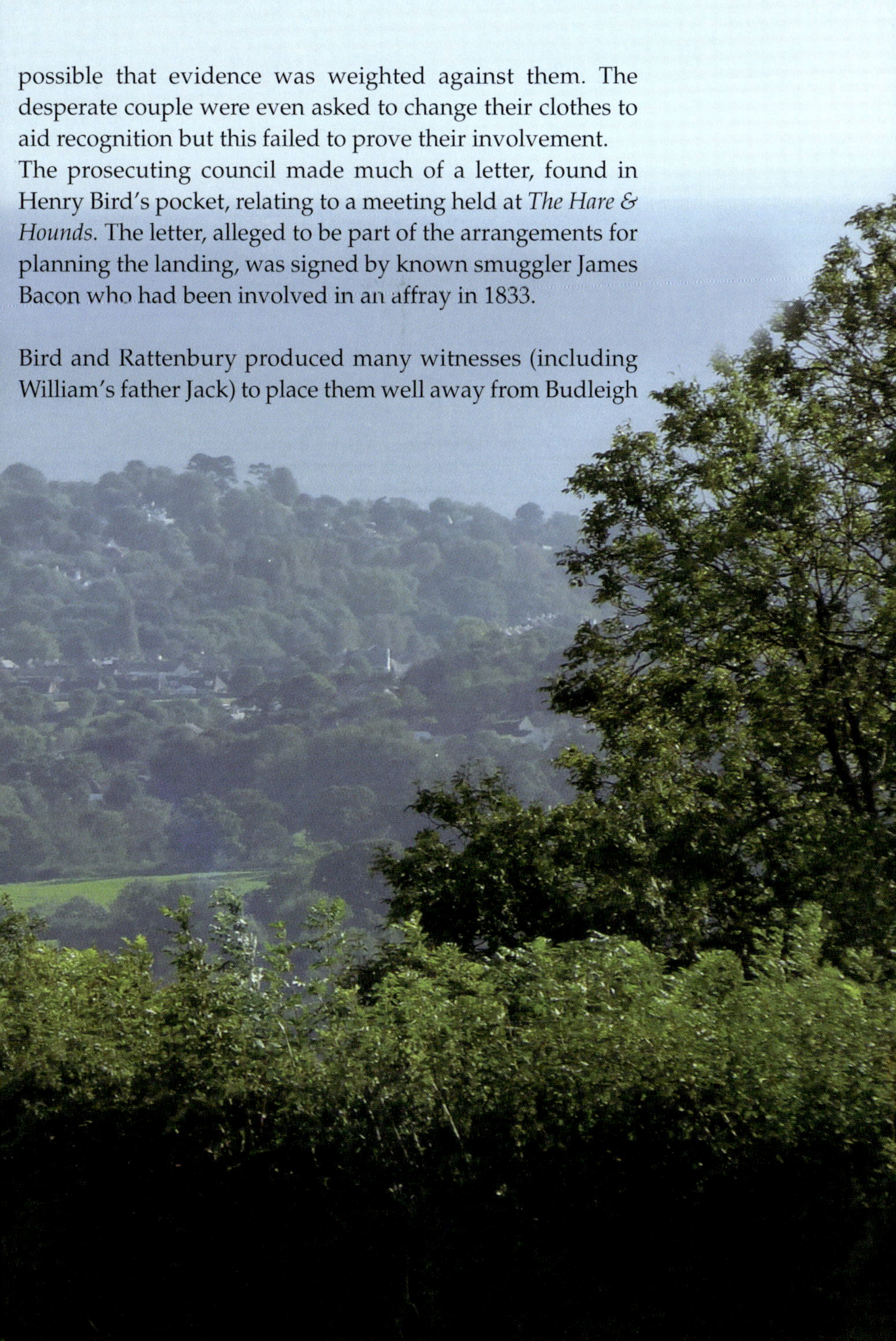

possible that evidence was weighted against them. The desperate couple were even asked to change their clothes to aid recognition but this failed to prove their involvement. The prosecuting council made much of a letter, found in Henry Bird's pocket, relating to a meeting held at *The Hare & Hounds*. The letter, alleged to be part of the arrangements for planning the landing, was signed by known smuggler James Bacon who had been involved in an affray in 1833.

Bird and Rattenbury produced many witnesses (including William's father Jack) to place them well away from Budleigh

on the night in question. These efforts proved to be in vain and both men were found guilty and sentenced to seven years transportation, but granted a Royal Pardon due to petitions made to the King. This was achieved partly by Jack Rattenbury calling at the house of Justice of the Peace, Captain John Carslake and appealing for mercy for his son *'who had been wrongfully taken up for smuggling'*. Could it be that Carslake was keen to ensure his future supplies of brandy?

The large stone at the front of the main building is part of Devonshire folklore. Legend says it dances at night when it hears the bells of Sidbury church, and that it rolls down the valley to drink at the River Sid – some say to wash away the blood-stains!

The Hare & Hounds was previously known as Hunters Lodge. Behind the whitewashed walls of this traditional Devon free house is a comfortable interior with wooden beams and winter log fires. Besides the daily carvery, the extensive menu includes classic pub dishes and snacks. Main course options include beef in Guinness with roast potatoes, as well as fish dishes and vegetarian options. The permanent cask ales are brewed less than 10 miles away at Ottery Brewery.

Although extended beyond recognition from the earlier building, interior clues to the original smugglers' pub remain, including massively thick walls in some areas and the huge inglenook with its bread oven.

At 249 feet above sea level there are commanding views from the pub garden for 6 miles down the valley to the villages of Sidbury and Sidford and beyond to the seaside town of Sidmouth on the English Channel.

On the regular route for smugglers, the twelfth-century packhorse bridge over the River Sid at Sidford was the site of a 1644 skirmish during the English Civil War.

The Blue Ball fronts the A3052 a couple of miles east of Bowd and a stone's throw from the Sidmouth to Honiton crossroads.

Sidford

The Blue Ball Inn

Stevens Cross, EX10 9QL

Tel: 01395 514062

www.blueballinnsidford.co.uk

The little River Sid runs its 6 mile course throughout formerly notorious smuggling country. From its source at the head of a small ravine near the Hare & Hounds (see page 60) it flows south through Sidbury and Sidford before spilling into the sea at Sidmouth.

Almost the whole community hereabouts was involved in free trading and family units could comprise generations of smugglers. In the Sid Valley, the names Bartlett, Northcote, Rattenbury, and Mutter occur frequently throughout the period and can still be traced around the area.

The village church of St Giles and St Peter at Sidbury was a convenient stopping off point for smugglers moving contra-

The pub has a history dating back to 1385 but was destroyed by fire in March 2006 and completely rebuilt by the following August.

band inland. During that time religious ceremonies, particularly weddings, were held in church porches near the door so as many people as possible could witness the proceedings. Some churches like Sidbury had a room above the porch known as a Parvis or Parvise where secret meetings were held.

Churches and churchyards were widely used for storing contraband and this was made easier when vicars who held more than one 'living' paid a nominal wage to a curate to officiate in their place. In 1736 John Sleech held the living of both Farringdon and Sidbury where he left his curate William Jenkins in charge. In 1785 Sleech was followed by William Carrington, also an absentee rector.

Sidford, in particular, played an important part in the free trading enterprise. Situated on roads leading to major towns and cities, it was well placed to funnel illicit contraband convoys. The Blue Ball Inn at Sidford was already 250 years old when a Civil War battle took place on and around the twelfth-century packhorse bridge. The original inn was destroyed by fire in March 2006 and rebuilt incorporating traditional materials of thatch, cob and flint with plenty of

The Blue Ball today is a spacious dining pub run with very friendly efficiency.
Below: Traditional materials were used in the rebuild to give it an authentic atmosphere.

When I called there were six real ales on tap all kept to 'Cask Marque' quality.

timber beams to restore the atmosphere of a bygone age. The Blue Ball today is a spacious dining pub run with very friendly efficiency. When I called there were six real ales on tap all kept to top quality 'Cask Marque' condition.

Dating from 1350, Sidmouth's famous old smugglers' pub the Ship is now a twenty first-century Costa Coffee House.

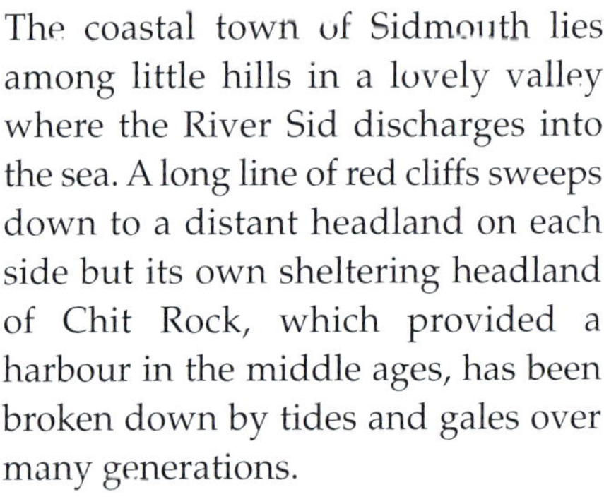

The coastal town of Sidmouth lies among little hills in a lovely valley where the River Sid discharges into the sea. A long line of red cliffs sweeps down to a distant headland on each side but its own sheltering headland of Chit Rock, which provided a harbour in the middle ages, has been broken down by tides and gales over many generations.

The former Old Ship Inn is a substantial building with cob walls almost 3 feet thick and was said to be once part of a monastery. It later became an inn, and one of the chief centres of smuggling in East Devon. A passage at the back linked with Church Path, which

The interior of the Ship still retains original features the Sidmouth smugglers would have known.

Below: Original roof timbers are a prominent feature in the upstairs coffee lounge.

Church Path, Sidmouth, leading from a passage at the back of the Ship, was a well-used smugglers' route.

in turn led to the parish church of St Giles and St Nicholas. From this may be deduced the close connection between church and contraband in the past. The inn provided extensive stables at the side and rear and farmers riding into Sidmouth market used it as a meeting place.

The old passage to Church Path was blocked off when licensing laws were introduced. At one time the inn became a notorious dosshouse. In one ground floor room vagrants cooked their own meals, and a large first floor room was their dormitory. According to the curiously named 'Dappy Pinn' the property once changed hands for 20 guineas with the money handed across the bar in a quick deal during a 'typical rowdy scene'. The centuries-old inn has now been transformed from a popular hostelry into a twenty-first-century coffee shop.
During re-decoration in June 1974, a secret room measuring 5′ x 3′ with a door 1′ wide was discovered behind a panel in an alcove in Beach House on Sidmouth Esplanade. The house, built in 1780, was originally known as Govier's Hall.

Incumbents at the parish church of St Giles and St Nicholas had a close connection with the smugglers.

Built in 1780, Beach House on Sidmouth Esplanade, was originally known as Govier's Hall, where a secret room was discovered in 1974.

In January 1833 George Parkes, the Sidmouth Coastguard together with another Preventive Officer from Budleigh Salterton attempted to stop a French smuggler landing his cargo of 100 kegs of brandy at Ladram Bay. They were overpowered by seventy men who had come to assist. The smugglers' leader – twenty-seven-year-old George Bacon – rushed Parkes who shot his pistol over the heads of the gang but the ball passed through the crown of another smuggler's hat.

The attack took place near the lodgings of Lord Rolles's gamekeeper, Mr Joslyn. Mrs Joslyn, seeing that Parkes was in a very bad way helped him light a blue flare to summon the station men at Sidmouth. Parkes was taken back to Sidmouth *'in a dangerous state with a cut hand and several broken ribs amongst other injuries'*.

On 23 March Bacon was committed for trial charged with assault and sentenced to seven years transportation. This was later commuted to two years imprisonment with hard labour.

One of the smugglers captured whilst carrying a pair of tubs was later impeached with several others residing in the neighbourhood. During their trial it was revealed sixty men had gathered at the house of John Miller at Woolbrook between Sidford and Bowd. Before heading for Otterton they waited in a field until dawn when they were called down to the beach to help with the unloading. The Sidford men were named as James Teed, blacksmith and Charles Musgrove, mason who were both fined £100. A third man Daniels was acquitted.

A long line of red cliffs at Sidmouth sweeps down to a distant headland on each side.

This handsome old smugglers' pub stand at the former contraband crossroads.

Bowd

The Bowd

Bowd Cross, Sidmouth EX10 0ND

Tel: 01395 513328

www.thebowdinn.co.uk

During the smuggling era the present day A3052 was already established as one of the most historic highways in Southern England, connecting the three significant seaports of Folkestone, Southampton and Exeter.

The junction at Bowd was a busy contraband crossroads. Goods landed at Ladram Bay 3 miles south were transported north across Mutter's Moor, passing the Bowd Inn and along well-worn smugglers' trails to Honiton. Mutter's Moor is named after smuggler Abraham Mutter remembered by sexton Robert Channon of Salcombe Regis as being *'more artful than Rattenbury'*.

Mutter from the hamlet of Harcombe, 3 miles east of Bowd, had a number of contraband storage pits just below Harcombe at Paccombe Bottom, owned a public house in Exmouth and was involved in the business of turf cutting on

The impressive external chimney with internal inglenook was added in 1657.
Below: Stone slab floors and exposed beams are a feature in this attractive thatched pub, with several comfortable seating and eating areas.

The Bowd is ultimately comfortable and welcoming.

the moor and wood cutting on nearby Peak Hill. Abraham Mutter, who initially worked with Rattenbury, owned several carts and a team of donkeys but Rattenbury is credited with the idea of hiding and conveying contraband under the legitimate loads of timber and turf.

Samuel Mutter, Abraham's sailor brother, stepped into Rattenbury's shoes when Jack was finally forced to retire due to recurring problems with gout. Samuel continued to provide the supplies for his enterprising brother Abraham, and later for Jack's son William, who had joined the smuggling gang. On coming of age, Abraham's son John also joined the family business, gaining the dubious honour of being the last man in the West Country to earn his living from smuggling.

The innocent activity of conveying turf and timber acted as a convenient cover for the transport and sale of contraband, especially since the biggest houses would consume large quantities of both fuel and brandy. Frequent visits by Mutter's carts and donkeys therefore aroused no suspicion.

The two regular beers are from the Otter Brewery in Honiton with a guest ale planned for the future.

Numerous stories surround the Mutter family, one telling how Sam Mutter was imprisoned in 1843 for smuggling, and how his release was eagerly anticipated by friends and family. However, the star guest at the welcome home party failed to appear. Fully three months passed before he appeared once more — with a cargo of contraband. The Mutters' involvement in smuggling ended when his fuel deliveries were superseded by the railway bringing cheap coal to the area.

Leading from the River Otter, sunken tracks like Passaford Lane provided extra concealment for smugglers moving contraband inland.

Dating from 1633, The Bowd Inn was originally an old cob farm house with adjoining barn and farmyard. The house had an open fire with smoke filtering out through a hole in the roof. The impressive external chimney with internal inglenook was added in 1657. Stone slab floors and exposed beams are a feature in this attractive thatched pub, with several comfortable seating and eating areas.

Mutter's Moor, just south of Bowd, where smuggler Abraham Mutter cut peat and timber.

Today The Bowd is a really popular family eatery offering traditional pub fare and renowned as a Sunday lunch venue for a great value carvery with a good choice of quality meats – booking is recommended. The efficient and friendly young staff are smart, helpful, smiling and polite. One customer recently posted the comment: *'They knew how to speak to customers, and never once called us "Guys".'*

Contraband was hidden in the bottom of Abraham Mutter's carts beneath legitimate loads of turf and timber.

For sunny days and evenings there is also a large garden. When I called two regular beers were on offer from the Otter Brewery in Honiton with a guest ale planned for the future.

Abraham Mutter's favoured contraband landing beach at Ladram Bay.

East Budleigh

Sir Walter Raleigh

22 High Street, East Budleigh EX9 7ED

Tel: 01395 442510

Prior to the early sixteenth century the River Otter was navigable as far as Otterton, the whole area being a scene of considerable activity. East Budleigh was a thriving town playing an important role in continental trade concerned with the production and dyeing of wool. Budley Haven, on the left bank was a port with an established shipbuilding industry. At the time Budleigh Salterton was a desolate empty place with a mere collection of huts used by workers panning for salt. Despite many valiant attempts to maintain navigation the River Otter gradually silted up and trade moved around the coast to the River Exe.

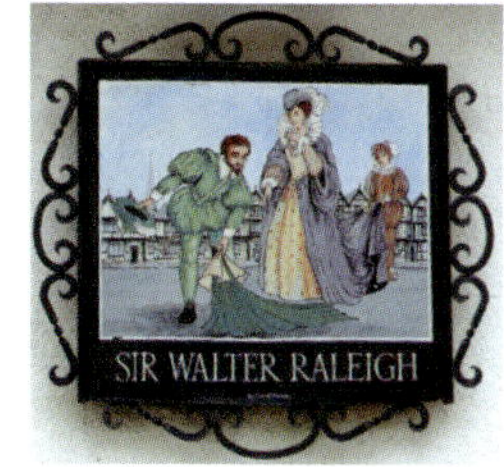

Named after East Budleigh's most famous son, the neatly thatched pub, is centrally situated along the quiet village street.

Affable landlord Jerry Fry is passionate about serving a perfect pint of real ale.

The two-room interior has a comfortable cottagey feel.

Today East Budleigh is a quiet village lying at the heart of 'Raleigh Country'. The renowned Elizabethan adventurer and writer Sir Walter Raleigh was born here at Hayes Barton in 1552. The Raleigh family had settled at East Budleigh in 1537 and involved themselves early in the village community. Walter's father was a church warden at All Saints and the oldest memorial in the church is to the memory of his first wife Joan. The Raleigh family pew, dated 1537, still stands on the left side of the nave.

Except for telegraph wires little has changed in this scene since the days of the smugglers.

The young Walter Raleigh received his early education at Vicar's Mead, down Hayes Lane opposite Hill Farm. Built in 1485 and, as the name implies, it was the Vicarage for many centuries. Matthew Mundy, vicar here for thirty-two years from 1741 was the sponsor of local smugglers and became a rich leaseholder with properties in East Budleigh and Otterton.

At this time contraband was secreted everywhere in and around the village including the Parish Room, now a bedroom in Vicar's Mead, whose thick walls conceal two secret passages, 18 inches wide leading to a cellar. There are also rumours that a tunnel led away from the house to the church. East Budleigh continued to be a centre for the distribution of smuggled goods when Mundy was succeeded in 1794 by Reverend Ambrose Stapleton. The following year Sir Henry

Standing prominently at the top of th High Street, All Saints church enjoys wonderful views across the village fr the churchyard. The Raleigh family pe can still be found in the nave.

Rolle purchased the manor and estates which included the gift of the church living. Both Mundy and Stapleton etched their names in a small pane of glass in the leaded-light window beside Vicar's Mead front porch.

Stapleton remained for fifty-eight years and was the last incumbent to reside at Vicar's Mead, living there until his death in 1852. He was a vigorous, kindly man who preached powerful sermons but had no conscience about inheriting the position of head of the lucrative illegal trade.

In addition, the 'Dissenters' who worshipped at Salem Chapel to the north of the village, were also enthusiastic free traders. Often deprived of their livelihood because of their religious beliefs, it is not surprising they were happy to embrace profitable smuggling opportunities. The two churches may have been divided in doctrine, but united in the trading of smuggled goods between the vicars of All Saints and the ministers at Salem Chapel.

Salem Chapel was built in 1719 of Beer stone and cob having a hipped slate roof with an interior central pillar supporting a vaulted plaster ceiling. The roof is unique

Vicar's Mead where young Raleigh attended school later became the rectory home for two consecutive smuggling vicars.

Salem Chapel where dissenting Minister Samuel Leat hid gin, cognac, tea, lace and silks in the attic.
Below: The single central beam supporting the roof of the chapel created a perfect void for concealing contraband above the ceiling.

with an inside concave ceiling forming a recessed well with a hidden trap door to an attic. A man standing in this well could not be seen, but had a clear view for miles around, making it an ideal lookout against approaching Customs Men.

The Minister from 1768 to 1807 was Samuel Leat who grew wealthy from smuggling. He allowed his associates to hide gin, cognac, tea, lace and silks in the chapel attic. Following Leat's death in 1817 a scandal developed involving embezzled funds and the suspected suppression of his will culminating in the desecration of his grave in May 1818 when the coffin was opened and his body mangled.

Originally known as King William IV, the name of this truly welcoming sixteenth-century country pub was later changed to The King's Arms. In 1967 it was changed again to the Sir Walter Raleigh after East Budleigh's most famous son. Set in the middle of the delightful village at the junction with Hayes Lane, leading to Raleigh's birthplace, the building formerly consisted of two cottages which were converted into a Jacobean-style pub towards the end of the eighteenth century. Many original features remain including wooden beams throughout the two separate areas. The old jug and bottle hatch can still be seen behind the bar and there are a couple of quirky alcoves whose purpose is unknown.

The Sir Walter Raleigh is a friendly free house run by a local family where owner Sally Miller supports her daughter Kristy Fry in the kitchen. Quality home cooked food is served lunchtimes and in the evenings. It is wise to reserve a table for evening dining and for Sunday lunch.

Kristy's husband Jerry runs the bar and cellar. A list of the next twenty real ales to be served is displayed on the wall beside the bar. Real cider from Green Valley is also available. The Sir Walter Raleigh is the hub of the village; the local book club regularly meets here as does the football club and church choir. As with all genuine pubs dogs on leads are welcome in the bar.

Birthplace and childhood home of Sir Walter Raleigh, Hayes Barton lies a mile west of the village centre.

SIR WALTER RALEIGH (1552-1618)
UNVEILED BY
HRH THE DUKE OF KENT KG
9 FEBRUARY 2006

The 2006 statue of Sir Walter Raleigh stands proudly outside the entrance to All Saints church.

Standing for centuries by the bridge over the River Clyst this ancient hostelry is a national treasure.

Topsham
Bridge Inn

Topsham, Exeter EX3 0QQ

Tel: 01392 873862

www.cheffers.co.uk

Topsham lies 3 miles southeast of the centre of Exeter, standing partly on the low shore of the Exe and partly on an isthmus between the great river and its tributary, the Clyst. From the late thirteenth century, construction of weirs in the River Exe by the Countess, and later Earls, of Devon compromised the prosperity of Exeter to the benefit of Topsham, owned by the Earls, and downstream of the obstructions.

Caroline Cheffers-Heard is from the fourth generation of the family to own and run the pub.

Topsham is mentioned throughout Jack Rattenbury's memoirs who along with his fellow smugglers certainly would have frequented the Bridge Inn. Rattenbury records spending the second half of 1798, *'fishing and smuggling'* before heading for Topsham.

'In February 1799, having been informed that a brig lying at Topsham required hands, I went to see the captain, whose name

was Elson, and agreed to go with him for £4 10s per month. By the end of March our vessel was ready for sea, and having a fair wind, we proceeded on our voyage.'

The vessel was the *Bickford*, a square-sterned brigantine owned by Topsham merchant James Jackson and William Bickford Jackson of Bideford.

On 28 July 1806, Captain Eales of the *Alarm* reported his oared boat useless and returned it to Topsham's Custom House store where it was later purchased by Jack Rattenbury who wrote:

'I went with three other men in an open boat to the islands [Channel Islands]. *We made two good voyages. We then bought an eight-oared boat which had belonged to the* Alarm *cutter, but had been condemned at the custom house. In this we succeeded very well'.*

Many a smugglers' conference must have taken place in the two small rooms and it's not difficult to imagine old time free traders occupying the high-backed settles.

The Bridge Inn, a national treasure of a pub stands beside the River Clyst where it curves gently around the back of the town. Needless to say, its out-of-the-way spot beside the marshes and away from the commercial quays made it a favourite haunt of smugglers.

There has been a dwelling on this site from the time of the Domesday Book but the present building is substantially sixteenth century. The actual date of the different parts vary considerably because the building grew progressively, with new rooms added as required. Most of the fabric is local stone, but the old brewhouse at the rear is traditional Devon cob. This has the remains of the hop drying floor, and is adjacent to a large brewing chimney.

Photographs along the corridor include those of the Queen's visit on 27 March 1988.

Spy holes in the shutters allowed free trading patrons to keep a lookout for Customs Officers and the Press Gang.

At busy times drinks are often served in this quirky corridor.

Modernity is missing here. There's no background music, no TV, no mobile phones, no job-lot repro 'antiques' no card transactions, no chips or burgers and no lager dispensing taps. Instead the Bridge has a long history of promoting real ale from local breweries and particularly famous for select ales from the rest of the country. Although the actual list varies from week to week there are usually eight or more cask conditioned beers dispensed straight from the keg. There are even special 'third' glasses enabling customers to sample a wider selection. There's no bar as such and staff nip up and down cellar steps and often serve drinks around the door into the corridor.

Local cider arrives from just a mile away and robust country wines don't have to travel much further. Locally sourced food (served at lunchtime only) includes pasties, granary ploughman's or sandwiches made from home-cooked ham with elderflower and gooseberry chutney.

Many a smugglers' conference must have taken place in the two small rooms. It's not difficult to imagine old time free traders seated on the high backed settles enjoying a glass of fiery spirits whilst smoking contraband tobacco in clay pipes and uttering threatening oaths against the local Customs Officer.

In fine weather customers take drinks outside to watch the bird life on the sludgy mudflats, and in bad weather the Old

There's no bar as such, just this small serving hatch.

In bad weather the Old Maltings acts as an overspill bar and occasional concert venue for folk and blues music.

Maltings acts as an overspill bar and occasional concert venue for folk and blues music.

The current licensee Caroline Cheffers-Heard, is the latest family member to run the pub since her great-grandfather William John Gibbings from Clyst St George bought it in 1897. On 27 March 1988 Queen Elizabeth II famously visited her first-ever pub, and this was it – a curious choice, as it is hardly representative. It was arranged after palace officials spotted the Bridge Inn's internet page and, impressed with its traditional village pub image they contacted Caroline asking if they could bring the Queen. When Her Majesty spoke to Caroline she complimented her on the resolve required to remain unchanging in an ever-changing world.

Picnic sets in the pub garden are perfectly placed for watching bird life on the sludgy mudflats of the Clyst.

Overlooking the Exe estuary, The Passage House has been trading for nearly three hundred years.

Topsham

The Passage House Inn

Ferry Road, Topsham EX3 0JN

Tel: 01392 873653

www.passagehouseinntopsham.co.uk

Topsham's location as a sheltered harbour allowed it to thrive as a port and as a centre for fishing and shipbuilding. During the smuggling era when the Exe was thronged with sailing vessels, Topsham boasted more than forty pubs. Its shipyards were major employers and at its height the commercial trade rivalled that of London.

By the Second World War that was all just a memory. Writing in 1954, Devon author W. G. Hoskins observed:

'Topsham is one of those ancient, decayed estuary ports which are perhaps the most fascinating kind of town England can

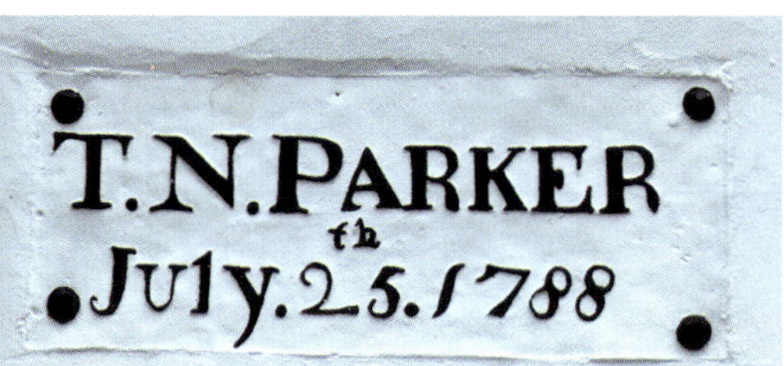

Mr Parker recorded his association with the inn sixty seven years after its original opening.

show, with their colour, smells and strong sense of past life everywhere in the streets and alleys along the waterfronts.'

To stroll along the waterfront streets of The Strand, Ferry Road and Fore Street is to discover that Hoskins' words are as true today as they were well over half a century ago. The perfect place to start is with a visit to Topsham Museum, housed in one of a group of late seventeenth-century buildings at 25 The Strand. An important aspect of the Museum's focus is Topsham's maritime history including its smuggling legacy. Visitors can also admire the furnished period rooms of the original house and the Sail Loft displaying the town's historical timeline.

A little further north in Fore Street, before it becomes Ferry Road, stands the Lighter Inn. Built in 1760 as the Custom House it grew to incorporate the former Harbour Master's house and Customs' lockup shed. The King's beam, used by Customs Officers to weigh imported goods still stands on the inn's forecourt. Seized tobacco was generally burned –

An excellent wine selection accompanies a great range of West Country real ales kept to 'cask marque' quality at The Passage House Inn.

This relaxed eighteenth-century pub is light and airy with a traditional beamed bar.
Below: Open all day, The Passage House enjoys a reputation for good food from sandwiches to their specialist seafood platters to share.

2025lbs of it at Topsham in 1770 for example – but condemned tea was usually forwarded to London for disposal. Spirits were secured in the Customs warehouse before being sold locally although this led to attempted break-ins.

Windows in the bar and dining room overlook the peaceful terrace and river moorings to the nature reserve beyond.

The peak years for smuggling in East Devon, as elsewhere were around 1782, when reports from the Commissioners of Excise to the Prime Minister listed 25 armed vessels of up to 100 tons with crews of up to 20 men conveying goods into the Exeter area. They estimated that 1,248,000 gallons of brandy and 806,400 lb of tea were brought in during the previous three years so that as much as 90% of tea and spirits consumed had been smuggled. No figures were given for tobacco.

During a single month in 1784 the *Alarm* Revenue Cutter seized nearly 1200 casks which can have been only a small fraction of what came ashore. A Customs sale at Topsham in 1787 included 1587 gallons of brandy, 694 of gin and 143 of rum. Although it was offered '*in small lots for family use only*', incognito representatives of Topsham's pub landlords would certainly have been among the bidders.

In the early 1800s one of Rattenbury's main adversaries was Lieutenant Daniel Miller, formidable revenue cutter captain and officer in the Impress Service. In April 1806, hearing a report that smugglers were off the coast near Teignmouth, Miller took his gang-boat and encountered a sloop called *Providence*. The smugglers escaped in their rowing boat but Miller captured the ship and its substantial cargo of 162 kegs of spirits which he impounded at the Topsham Custom House.

'Topsham is one of those ancient, decayed estuary ports which are perhaps the most fascinating kind of town England can show.'

After the kegs were sold Miller submitted a claim for his share of profits. However, his senior officer Captain Mitchell, although not involved in the seizure, also made a claim.

Topsham Museum is housed in one of a group of late seventeenth-century buildings at 25 The Strand.

Miller being greatly vexed wrote to the Collector at Exeter quoting relevant passages from revenue laws successfully citing precedents and excluding Mitchell from the windfall. With two Royal Naval officers fighting over the substantial rewards of smuggling, Rattenbury's description of them and other seizing officers as *'harpies'* is no exaggeration – they stood to gain as much from smuggling as the smugglers themselves!

A plaque beside the front door of The Passage House dated 25 July 1788 bears the name T. N. Parker. Because it was actually built sixty-seven years earlier this could refer to a time when the pub was renovated or extended. Originally known as The Ferry Inn, it occupied only the southern end of the present building. By 1822 the name had been changed to The Passage House when Jabez Ireland was listed as the victualler and Ferry Road became known as Lower Passage Lane. From the twelfth century this route had been taken by monks using the ferry to travel between their monasteries across the South West.

This relaxed eighteenth-century pub features a traditional beamed bar with a slate-floored lower dining area. Windows in the bar and dining room overlook the peaceful terrace and river moorings to the nature reserve beyond, especially beautiful at sunset.

Open all day, The Passage House enjoys a reputation for good food from sandwiches to their specialist seafood platters to share, comprising smoked salmon, fresh crab, mussels, whitebait, garlic king prawns, wholetail scampi and smoked mackerel served with crusty bread. In addition to an excellent wine selection there is great range of west country real ales kept to 'cask marque' quality.

The Lighter Inn was formerly the Customs House. The King's Beam, *(seen on the left of the picture)* was used to weigh and assess duty on imported goods.

The Mount Pleasant Inn was first mentioned in 1756 but is almost certainly much older.

Dawlish Warren

Mount Pleasant Inn

Mount Pleasant Road, Dawlish Warren EX7 0NA

Tel: 01626 863151

www.mountpleasantinn.com

Dawlish Warren, at the mouth of the River Exe, overlooks a 2 mile broad channel where sea and river meet. Dawlish Warren is now a holiday centre with chalet parks, caravan sites and funfairs extending around it in all directions. During the smuggling era, however, it was a desolate place, a wide stretch of sand almost awash at high water, heaped up in dunes and overgrown with tussocks of coarse grasses.

In this island waste there were no roads or tracks at all and few people ever came to disturb the curlews or sea birds nesting unafraid. It was pleasant in daytime but dangerous at night and until the railway arrived, the warren was virtually a no-go area; a hide-out for villains, brigands and highwaymen of all sorts, quite apart from smugglers who found such wild conditions highly convenient for their nefarious business.

The main part of the inn comprises two large open-plan heavily-beamed linked rooms where a wide choice of favourite home-cooked food is served. **Below:** Fully carpeted and comfortably furnished lounge/dining areas boast outstanding sea views.

When it was deemed safe, free traders ran their boats ashore on the golden sands in the lee of Langstone Point. Contraband was conveyed to the Mount Pleasant Inn, an unpretentious beer house, perched picturesquely above undergrowth on the crest of an inland red sandstone bluff rising sheer from the marshy meadows.

The well kept West Country ales are from Otter and St Austell.

For smugglers the inn was a very convenient receiving house and signal station as it had caverns hollowed from the red sandstone in places inaccessible to the authorities. From its isolated elevation overlooking the flats, free traders could easily communicate encouragement or warning to friends anxiously riding at anchor out at sea.

Smugglers sailing into the Exe enjoyed the advantage shared by anyone landing goods at an estuary: once the land-guard was located, cargo could be run on the opposite shore, safe in the knowledge that the lowest bridging point was a long ride upstream. Signalling with a lantern from the pub windows, indicated which side of the estuary was safe, and bribing the ferryman or getting him drunk was a useful additional precaution.

On bord ye Revenue Cutter
Elizabeth – September ye 23
1774/-

Your Lordships –

With Regard to ye late epidemic of Unlawful Contraband Running from Roskoff/- Reliable informants have brought it to our ears that certain cargoes – namely 50 half anker tubs of Choice Brandy have been covertly landed after nightfall upon ye sands at Dawlish Spit and thence delivered to the Mount Pleasant hostelry close upon ye shore/- It is further disclosed that the casks are then secreted away within Several Ingenious Hiding Places within the fabric of the aforesaid House/-

Therefore – With Your Lordships consent it is my intention to place a discreet watch upon the said premises in order that we might apprehend these Evil Doers/-

I trust that my actions may meet with Your Lordships full approbation –

Your Humble Servant
Henry Lucas

Capt – Light Dragoons/.

Among the display of historical photographs and documents is this letter written on 23 September 1774 by Henry Lucas, a captain in the Light Dragoons.

With its expansive sea views the Mount Pleasant Inn still stands above the Dawlish Warren marshlands.

The inn as smugglers would have known it perched picturesquely above undergrowth on the crest of an inland red sandstone bluff rising sheer from the marshy meadows.

Among the many historic photographs and items displayed on the bar wall is this wonderful letter from Henry Lucas, a captain of the Light Dragoons, written in September 1774:

On board ye Revenue Cutter Elizabeth
September ye 23 1774.

Your Lordships,

With regard to ye late epidemic of Unlawful Contraband Running from Roskoff. Reliable informants have brought it to our ears that certain cargoes – namely 50 half anker tubs of Choice Brandy have been covertly landed after nightfall upon ye sands at Dawlish Spit and thence delivered to the Mount Pleasant hostelry close upon the shore.

It is further disclosed that the casks are then secreted away within Several Ingenious Hiding Places within the fabric of the aforesaid House.

Two hundred years ago the inn was headquarters of a notorious smuggling gang who stored contraband in tunnels and cellars beneath the building. During the Edwardian period the superbly ramshackle thatched, tile-hung hostelry traded as a tea garden.

Over the years the inn has been greatly extended and partly rebuilt following a series of fires.
Below: In the early 1880s, the inn was the venue for the Mount Pleasant Races and attracted excursions from far and wide.

Therefore – with your Lordships consent it is my intention to place a discreet watch upon the said premises in order that we might apprehend these Evil Doers.

I trust that my actions may meet with Your Lordships full approbation.

Your Humble Servant
Henry Lucas
Capt – Light Dragoons

Though greatly extended and partly rebuilt following a series of fires the Mount Pleasant Inn, with its expansive sea views, still stands high above the Dawlish Warren marshlands. Two hundred years ago the inn was headquarters of a notorious smuggling gang who stored their contraband in tunnels and cellars beneath the building. One longer tunnel is said to have led down to the beach.

The inn existed before 1756 and for the past two decades has been in the hands of one family. The Mount Pleasant Inn and surrounding area have been transformed beyond recognition. Views from the dining room windows look across chalet parks, caravan sites and funfairs to the line of low red rock cliffs that sweep around the bay.

The main part of the inn comprises two large open-plan heavily-beamed linked rooms. Fully carpeted and comfortably furnished these lounge/dining areas boast outstanding sea views. There is a wide choice of favourite home-cooked food including children's dishes. The well-kept West Country ales are from Otter and St Austell.

The Smugglers Inn stands boldly beside the A379 halfway between Dawlish and Teignmouth.

Holcombe

Smugglers Inn

27 Teignmouth Road, Dawlish EX7 0LA

Tel: 01626 862301

www.thesmugglersinn.net

Sitting halfway between Dawlish and Teignmouth the seaside settlement of Holcombe is bisected by the busy A379 with the oldest part of the village lying west of the highway where picturesque cob and thatched cottages have for decades been an attraction for artists.

A full lunch and evening menu is served every day of the week in the large rear dining room extension alongside the pub's famous 'Farmers Feast Carvery'.

The oldest part of the pub has been refurbished to produce a comfortable lounge and bar.

Dartmoor Legend and Teignworthy Reel are the house beers with a guest ale changing on a regular basis.

On the far side of the main road a track called Smugglers Lane still leads down to a cove whose seclusion – and suitability for landing contraband – was rudely shattered with the building of the railway.

Early photographs show The Country House Inn before and after it was renamed and rebranded the Smugglers Inn – an appropriate name given the occupation of a number of its clientele. Originally Holcombe smugglers had operated from a pub called The Lobster Inn further down hill near Smug-

Seats on the raised rear terrace afford panoramic views of the ocean and surrounding countryside.

glers Lane, a well used trail leading down to the landing beach accessible by horse transport.

In the garden of The Lobster was the concealed entrance to a tunnel which led down to a huge cave opposite the Parson and Clerk rocks. At night a man holding a light and standing in the cave mouth could signal a warning or an all clear to colleagues out at sea. The protruding cliffs on either side screened him from the Coastguards' view in either direction at Dawlish and Teignmouth. It seems probable the cave and tunnel provided storage with the adjacent track used at safe times for moving contraband inland.

This venerable old hostelry was initially called 'The Country House Inn'. The unmade road has since been surfaced, realigned and widened taking it further away from the pub.

In 1819, when first recorded in the rate books, The Lobster Inn and surrounding land were owned by the Pennel family. Mr. Edwin Pennel, added the much larger private house of Sunnylands to the front of the inn, and the coat of arms of Pennel's brother, who had been Consul General of Brazil, still adorns the roadside elevation.

By 1842 Sunnylands was owned by Mr Oliver Mainwaring Matthews who, with Mr William Ferris, also owned the brewery in Dawlish. Both men shared a financial interest in a cluster of cottages in the village comprising 'Lobsters, Lobster Cottage and End Cottage'. It is thought when Mainwaring sold Sunnylands these combined cottages became the new

At the beginning of the twentieth-century the pub was renamed and rebranded the Smugglers Inn to reflect its early history.

Right:
Holcombe smugglers originally operated from The Lobster Inn, seen in the foreground, now part of a large family house called Sunnylands.

'Lobster Inn' for a short period. Around this time the much larger Country House Inn was built further up the hill alongside the turnpike road.

Free trading was almost at an end in 1846, when Isambard Kingdom Brunel sealed off the seaward end of the smugglers' tunnel with an iron grill, as part of building works extending the Exeter to Dawlish line of the South Devon Railway. Thirty years later the SDR was amalgamated with the Great Western Railway which follows the River Exe to Dawlish Warren running beneath the sea cliffs to Teignmouth, then accompanying the River Teign to Newton Abbot following tidal waters for about 13 miles, 4 of which are open sea.

The figure in the photograph is approaching Lobsters, which together with the adjoining Lobster Cottage and End Cottage became the smugglers' drinking den for a while after Sunnylands was sold.

The original Country House Inn now constitutes about 25% of the present building and has been refurbished to provide a spacious lounge bar area. The main restaurant is a later extension where a full lunch and evening menu is available every day of the week alongside the pub's famous 'Farmers Feast Carvery'.

In addition to a full wine list the Smugglers Inn offers a number of choice real ales including Dartmoor Legend, Teignworthy Reel and a regularly varying guest beer. Seats on the raised rear terrace afford panoramic views of the ocean and surrounding countryside.

This contemporary print shows smugglers landing contraband near the Parson and Clerk rocks before hauling it up the trail now known as Smugglers Lane. (Courtesy of Devon archives).

Below: Screened from view by protruding cliffs on either side a man in the cave mouth could safely signal with a light to colleagues out at sea.

Ye Olde Jolly Sailor is found halfway along Northumberland Avenue, set back from the later building line by a spacious forecourt area.

Ye Olde Jolly Sailor
Teignmouth

46 Northumberland Place, Teignmouth TQ14 8DE

Tel: 01626 772864

We have now reached the northern bank of the River Teign, 14 miles from Exeter and the southern extent of the city's Custom House jurisdiction. The town suffered a devastating invasion by the French in 1690, earning the dubious distinction of being the site of the last foreign invasion on English soil. The French used the Jolly Sailor as their headquarters and accordingly it is one of the oldest buildings left standing.

An ale house has been on this site in some form since 1132.

By the eighteenth century it had begun to reinvent itself aided partly by funds derived from trade in contraband goods purchased from its former enemy. When the railway opened up the coast in the 1840s, Teignmouth became the second most popular health resort in Devon. Previous trades of salt production, fishing, boat building and free trading gave way to the demands of tourism. As local business increased so did waterway traffic. Clay and granite quarried nearby were important exports. The Quay is constructed from this local granite.

The cosy and comfortable interior consists essentially of three areas with beamed ceilings, stone walls, open fireplaces and perimeter banquette seating with tables.

This is a delightful family run traditional waterside pub where quality local cask ales and fresh, homemade food are much enjoyed.

In the late eighteenth century, privateering was common in Teignmouth, as in other West Country ports. Teignmouth investors fitted out two privateers: *The Dragon* with 16 guns and 70 men; and *The Bellona*, described as carrying *'16 guns, 4 cohorns and 8 swivels'*. She set sail on her first voyage in September 1779, and was *'oversett in a violent Gust of Wind'* off Dawlish with the loss of 25 crew members.

Also in 1779 the French ship *L'Emulation* with a cargo of sugar, coffee and cotton was offered for sale at 'Rendle's Great Sale Room' in the town and this provocative newspaper advertisement for *The Dragon* appeared:

In past times this chimney incorporated a 'priest hole' to shelter Catholic clerics in fear of persecution.

There are picnic tables on the beach and a further rear patio features floral hanging baskets.
Below: The pub's setting affords views across the fish quay with boats in the estuary.

The pub was formerly known as The Ferryboat after the river crossing service still operating between Shaldon and Teignmouth.

A new advantageous Plan of Privateering For a Six Months Cruize. All Gentlemen Seamen and Able Landmen who delight in the Music of Great Guns and distressing the Enemies of Great Britain have now a fine opportunity of making their Fortunes by entering on Board The Dragon Privateer ... now ready to be launch'd in the Harbour of Teignmouth... Any persons capable of beating a Drum or blowing a French horn shall have great encouragement.

The free trade era is also commemorated at Shaldon on the south side of the Teign estuary, facing Teignmouth. The sheltered estuary was a favoured landing spot, and a smugglers' tunnel cuts through the cliff, leading to Shaldon beach.

Halfway along Northumberland Avenue, set back from the later building line by a spacious forecourt, stands Ye Olde Jolly Sailor formerly known as The Ferryboat, as for centuries

Sheltered beneath the headland of The Ness, Shaldon's red sand beach was a favourite contraband landing site.

the ferry from Shaldon landed regularly where the fish quay now stands. Records in Exeter indicate there has been an ale house on this site in some form since 1132.

Ye Olde Jolly Sailor is a delightful family-run traditional waterside pub where quality local cask ales and fresh, homemade food can be enjoyed. The cosy, comfortable interior is essentially three areas with beamed ceilings, stone walls, open fireplaces and perimeter banquette seating with tables.

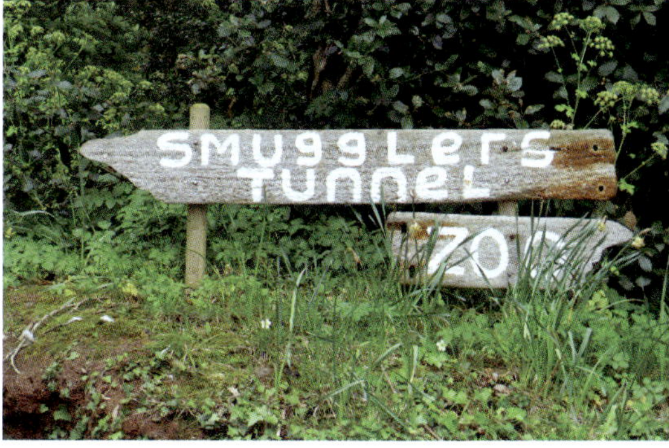

An old smugglers' trail leads to the beach.

The fireplace in the lower area now houses a wood burner. In past times the chimney incorporated a 'priest hole' to shelter clerics in fear of persecution. When Queen Elizabeth I came to the throne in 1558, several Catholic plots were devised to remove her and severe measures were taken against priests. At the rear is a further patio with floral hanging baskets, a sheltered smokers' retreat adorned by a relief mural of the 'Ness' headland, plus views across the fish quay with boats in the estuary and Shaldon's shoreline as a backdrop.

Shaldon's beach is accessed via a tunnel cut through the cliffs.

Selected Bibliography

Gerald Gosling, *Exe to Axe – The Story of East Devon*

Eileen Hathaway, *Smuggler – John Rattenbury and his Adventures in Devon and Cornwall 1778-1844*

Richard Platt, *Smugglers' Britain*

Mary Waugh, *Smuggling in Devon & Cornwall*

Free trading was almost at an end in 1846 when Isambard Kingdom Brunel sealed off the sea end of the Holcombe smugglers' tunnel as part of building works extending the Exeter to Dawlish line of the South Devon Railway.